The Quantum Side of Addiction

By

Joe Frank Stokes Jr.

Life choices so many times more than often are based on past seeds of horror stories. We can't heal that way. Life is about exploring new and endless possibilities of LOVE and ABUNDANCE. Take the journey with me as we dig into "THE CPU OF THE GODS," "THE MIND." That's what Life is all about; that's what this is all about.

Venture with me... Here at THE QUANTUM SIDE.

-- Joe Frank Stokes Jr

(*YouTube Channel* -----"The Quantum Side of Addiction")

THE QUANTUM SIDE OF ADDICTION HELPS YOU FEEL EMPOWERED, TAKE RESPONSIBILITY FOR YOUR LIFE, BECOME COMMITTED TO STAYING SOBER, HEALTHY, AND HAPPY, AND START ENJOYING YOUR LIFE.

IT HELPS YOU TO FEEL IN CONTROL AND ON THE RIGHT PATH. I WOULD RECOMMEND IT TO ANYONE SUFFERING FROM ADDICTION, ANXIETY, OR UNHAPPINESS.

Joseph R. Rizza

THE QUANTUM SIDE OF ADDICTION HAS BEEN FULL OF INFORMATION THAT I'VE BEEN ASCERTAINING THROUGHOUT MY RECOVERY. IT HAS GIVEN ME A NEW SENSE OF HOPE WHICH I WASN'T SURE IF I'D EVER GET BACK.

I'VE HAD GREAT SUCCESS IN MAINTAINING MY SOBRIETY, AND I OWE IT ALL TO THE VIEWS OF FRANK STOKES.

Gloria Lynn

Table of Contents

Introduction

Starting off this book, let me say that what I am doing is unique. The views of this book are not similar to those of NA or AA. A different new mindset will be opened and expressed. You no longer need the person you were. Please leave them in your past and forget them forever. In your mind, I want you to see that person dying and no longer physically alive. I want you to see yourself emerging as a new entity that will do nothing but work to transcend in life.

This book is going to shed light on your existence. You are about to find out who you are. You're about to learn how to change your life and live the way you were meant to live; stop living the way you were programmed and start living the way you want. You're about to know who is really in charge.

The Quantum Side is a new way of living and thinking. A new way of being. Your old life is now just a movie you can watch on the screen of your past. It's time to upgrade! The Quantum Side is all about feeling happy and fulfilled with life, getting in touch with your true inner self, and achieving your goals so you can live the best life possible.

From this point on, you are a new person. A new program is about to be installed on your hard drive. And when you are rebooted, you will move in a new direction. You're going to have a new habit, a new method, a new existence, new energy, and at last, a new purpose. The best part is that this program is like a magnet; the more you get closer to it, the more you will get engulfed in its all-positive magnetic field. You take one step, and the remarkable results will encourage you to run along this path to a new you.

Following this book doesn't mean you will have to work hard and look for your new life. Instead, the new life you want will find you and seek you out. And no matter where you hide, as long as you see it, feel it and believe it, it will seek you out because it has a gift for you. The gift of a new life. This magnetic force will propel the gift giver is working now as we speak. And it's figuring out the fastest route to get you carrying the most gifts. Sounds good!

But there are enemies of this energy. The common enemies. The same ones that have whispered in your ear all of your life. Doubt, hate, insecurities, self-sabotage, and mental weakness. Aside from all these, fear is the number one enemy of our success. But don't worry. We'll get to the bottom of them and pull them from the roots.

When you start this journey, try not to focus on the rewards; focus on yourself and your life. The most crucial part of every journey is the focus. Whenever you start focusing on the reward, you become restless and lose interest in the journey. You always look for rewards at the expense of work. So, focus on making your life better, and remember that this journey's gifts won't be at the end. They will be given along the way. You wouldn't have to look for them. You only need to prepare, get excited, and, most importantly, get a clear vision. And build on it. You'll need it like water to make it out alive.

The quantum side is a realm of infinite possibilities, so its interpretation varies from person to person. If you try to tap into this realm by following someone else entirely, you won't get the desired results. So, I will only guide you toward your goal, and you will cover the distance. In this book, I'll be going into as much as possible without too much detail.

This book is a revolutionary, new type of self-help book that not only helps you change your life but also helps you change your brain. The Quantum Side was created to help you break free from old habits, commit to your goals, and live a better life. It's made for the person who has taken the first step in their journey with their eyes wide open and ready to take on the world.

In the upcoming chapters, I will be giving you insight into your power of the mind and your power of manifestation. I will list and describe the laws and principles of this universe so that you move according to them to get everything you desire.

You won't find any similarity between this book and NA or AA. Remember those long unnecessary stories you used to hear and tell? Forget them. Please do your best to forget them. And never say them again. Or at least for the next ten to 20 years.

Those stories didn't do you any good, and they never will. Our brain does not get significant learning from stories; it doesn't work like that. And these tired, long, half-truth, half-fairy tale stories of addiction hold you hostage in the prison that you create brick by brick, story by story. I will explain how the mind and imagination work and what things you should be imagining and repeating again and again.

On this journey to a better life, you are the driver of your life; you are in control. The only thing you require before starting this journey is to be ready, physically and mentally. It would be best if you had an image of a child again; this imagination will guide you to the Promised Land.

This book doesn't subscribe to any religion. I'm not a believer in anything that holds your mind hostage. I believe in my true self. I believe in the profound power inside us.

Unlike the religions, what I'll be sharing is solely up to you. I will share how you can tap into your inner power of manifestation and creation. I will be encouraging you to become the sole controller of your destiny. However, I will guide you to form a connection with a universal source of power, a realm filled with infinite possibilities, the thing I call THE SOURCE or THE VORTEX.

The other programs, such as NA and AA, advertise themselves by stating that their relapse rate is 85%. However, you will find that the opposite of this is true. The rate of people who never return to these programs is 85%, meaning these programs can't be counted as successful.

So, the question is, what are we missing in this world of addiction in our fight against it? What we are missing is something new. This is needed to transform and reorganize our brain cells, make new connections, and bridge the gap between the world we want to be in and the world we are currently in. I will be helping you to transform your mind and incorporate these laws into your daily lives because these are essential to the structure of belief systems.

Like the Bible and many other books designed to increase our lives with guidance and wisdom, these laws are universal and apply to a belief system that, regardless of believing or not, still applies and will reap its effects on those unaware.

The concept behind these laws and principles is that when a thought arises in our mind, it produces an electrical field, and the feelings inside us produce a magnetic field. So, our body works as a broadcasting station for our thoughts and feelings, emitting electric and magnetic signatures. These signals affect and influence every aspect of our life.

This energy of your thoughts that you have been holding on to all your life has placed you where you are today and what powers you have. So, like it or not, you can't get to a place you desire if you can't defeat yourself and if you can't do your program.

Notice the word "Program"? What is it? A program is a set of related measures or activities with a particular long-term aim to a series of coded software instructions and to control the operation of a computer or other machines. For now, let's focus on the latter. The second part, the action part, states that a program provides a CPU or other machine with coded instructions for the automatic performance of a task to arrange according to a plan or schedule. Similarly, human beings act like computers, and these programs instruct automatic performance.

Do you agree that children between the ages of two to six absorb anything they see and hear? This is because they are ready to be programmed and believe they can follow any instructions, no matter how hard or easy the task is.

So you see, these two tools are essential. "Being Ready" and "Believing" before you enter the Quantum Side.

I cannot stress enough that first, you must forget your past NA or AA testimonies or stories that, sadly, you know by heart and all your friends know. We will be rewriting our futures based on nothing from our past but everything we can imagine in our abundant future. What we will be learning is the power of thinking big. The power to make is not from what we see or can touch with our hands or eyes but what we think in our minds and create from the electric and magnetic fields we project from our hearts and brains. This will be our canvas. This is where the creation starts and finishes.

The ultimate goal of this book is not to stop using drugs. That's a given. We all know the effects drugs have on us. It's a living nightmare. A dummy can figure that out. You can't make it with that monkey on your back. The ultimate goal of this book is to attain transformation, to take the control back into your hands.

Finally, before moving on, remember the two things you must do to make this book work; number one, you must believe, and number two, never give up. Until and unless you believe in yourself and are trying, you have all the power to attain your desire, and the moment you lose the belief, you get sucked into the darkness. So believing in yourself is the light you must always hold for a bright present and future.

The Power of the Mind and Imagination

Addiction is not a character flaw or a sign of weakness, so it requires more than resolve. Addiction can cause brain alterations, resulting in overwhelming cravings, making abstinence seem to be an unreachable objective.

"Healing is never too late." This phrase had us procrastinating instead of taking action at the very moment. Please stop believing "It's Never Too Late" because this statement is delusional. There are graveyards and prisons with millions of victims who thought they had one more in them but didn't. The most important part of this chapter is knowing "The Time Is Now" and "It Must Be Done Immediately" because you are already "Late." So, this is a major makeup time. Every second counts, and there is no more time to waste.

Once we are clean and ready to break the bad habit, confidence and belief are the most challenging to maintain. When we believe in ourselves, we activate various psychological processes that help us accomplish our objectives, achieve our aspirations, and improve our well-being. However, the inverse is also true. When we lack self-confidence or believe in ourselves, we are less willing to act, change, or try to improve things.

I have chosen this chapter to be the first in the book because it is the first and the essential step in your journey against addiction. Throughout our life, we make many decisions to change ourselves and certain parts of our life. This decision is the most challenging step because accepting that you require change is always challenging. However, for combating addiction, the scenario changes. Almost everyone knows and acknowledges that addiction is bad for them, and they need to change this habit. Even deciding to get rid of it over and over again.

Still, they always fall short of accomplishing their goal. And this shortcoming is their belief in themselves.

Beliefs can provide us with support, empower us, and lead us in our everyday choices. They can also constrain us and undermine our natural impulses for pleasure and success. So, the first step is thinking about staying away from addiction.

To understand this concept further, let's examine a scenario. Imagine that you are out of shape. You overcome this by joining a gym, exercising, and limiting your food consumption. You will be highly motivated to accomplish your goal for the first few days. You will regularly exercise and consume healthy food. But after a few days, you will see that you are not experiencing a significant change. This notion will be a massive blow to your belief and motivation. Ultimately, you will be back to your previous life.

You may look in the mirror and say, "You know what, this isn't working, it's not working." This notion will generate more failures and setbacks than anything else.

Believing in yourself is similar to turning the ignition key and starting the automobile. We can't go anywhere without it. We can't go ahead no matter how hard we try since our ideas, emotions, and behaviors aren't in sync with our objectives. So we either don't accomplish what we need to do, or we sabotage ourselves along the road, sometimes in obvious ways and sometimes in ways we're completely unaware of.

§

What Is Belief And What Affects It?

Before we move on to the "Law of Belief," we first need to understand the reality of beliefs and how they develop into our personalities. Beliefs are based on a combination of factual and fanciful viewpoints about life, ourselves, and other.

Beliefs are filters based on our experiences and the reality we perceive. They filter out everything that does not match our psychological conditioning from our sensory standpoint. As a result, we don't view reality as it is but as we perceive it.

Beliefs are founded on incomplete and skewed sensory perceptions conditioned and programmed through time by our recollections of prior events, situations, and experiences. These memories, which we feel are genuine, are only interpretations of reality at the moment. Similarly, over time, these interpretations of reality have been filtered through our belief systems and taken on a life of their own, reinterpreting our life experiences in a plethora of unique and creative ways that have little to do with the fact of those occurrences.

Our emotional state, frame of mind, social situation, and other elements influence how we perceive life's events and situations. If, for example, we have an emotional breakdown as certain events and circumstances occur around us, our views about those events and circumstances will be substantially different than if we were in a positive state of mind.

The belief system rejects any information that seems to be inconsistent or conflicting. As a result, it isn't easy to persuade someone if they have already formed a solid alternative idea regarding the material you are supplying them with.

The more emotionally involved a person is with a belief, the greater the conviction and the more unwavering this person's viewpoint will be. Consequently, they will reject any information, no matter how rational it seems, if it does not consistently align with their conditioned belief patterns.

When we prejudge anything, we draw unproductive assumptions about the events and situations directing our attention. In many cases, we form judgments despite contradictory facts or our best attempts to make rational sense of the circumstances.

Beliefs shape the strength of our emotional reactions to people, events, and situations. In other words, your beliefs supply you with pre-programmed core principles and emotional reactions that you engage when particular anchors in your environment get activated, causing specific and conditioned emotional responses.

Our beliefs determine our everyday actions. We continuously behave in line with our ideas about the world, ourselves, others, events, and situations. We have trained ourselves to accept these pre-programmed behaviors and responses without inquiry. And the longer we allow these conditioned reactions to persist in our minds, the more difficult it will be to change these patterns for the better.

Beliefs are nothing more than delusory representations of reality. This means that we control our reality through the means of our beliefs.

Law of Belief

According to the Law of Belief, whatever you believe with passion and conviction becomes your reality. You cannot begin to alter your reality or your performance unless you change your beliefs.

Another way to express this commandment is in the context of religion. All of the world's religions constantly emphasize the capacity to retain faith as a key to happiness and prosperity. Whether you accept religious doctrine or not, the Law of Belief may either aid or hinder your achievement, depending on whether you live in line with the Law.

You've probably heard the cynics and skeptics constantly saying, "I'll believe it when I see it!" In truth, it is the other way around; you will not see it until you believe it, no matter what "it" is!

Self-limiting thoughts are possibly the most damaging. These thoughts will prevent you from achieving your desires by making you feel that you are not capable.

"Whether you believe you can or can't, you're right!" This proverb is entirely consistent with the Law of Belief. Let me explain the following hypothetical situation:

You are a candidate for a job promotion. You have worked hard and think you are prepared, but you do not believe you will get promoted. Perhaps you believe other applicants are better or more competent. You might think you are indispensable at your present position (which is a mistake) or have some other harmful thinking habits. If you believe these things, it is practically certain that you will not be promoted. Why? Because your self-limiting beliefs will work together to keep you stuck!

When understood and implemented, the Law of Belief can assist anybody in manifesting the things in life that they genuinely want. The secret is to have complete clarity on your goals. This is a very effective way to achieve your goals and to feel that you are meant to accomplish them. You must constantly reaffirm this concept in your mind as time passes.

Re-examining the Universal Law of Attraction is another method to comprehend this Universal Law of Belief. When you have doubts or are afraid, your mind produces more uncertainty and confusion, creating additional anxiety. As you let go of fear, knowing you are loved, you feel more cherished and attract more love and pleasure.

If you believe all relationships are characterized by stress, emotional suffering, and a lack of resources. In that case, this is precisely the kind of connection you will attract.

Please allow me to clarify this for you for a moment. The Law of Belief does not suggest that you can expect Divine Source or Angels to suddenly appear at your doorstep and deliver everything without doing your part. You are led every step of the way.

The Law of belief says that anything you do becomes part of the unfolding of all you wish. This is because you believe and have confidence that this is the truth for you.

One of the most challenging things is to continue and stay focused on your objectives in the face of insurmountable setbacks or impediments. The intriguing thing about these situations is that we tend to perceive the world through a very limited lens, which is that barriers are bad. In reality, challenges are beneficial for us as they help us grow. We don't realize until much later that whatever the setback was, it was there for a purpose. And so, we have grown from that experience.

The main idea you need to remember is that we can reach our objectives by retaining faith and living in line with the Law of Belief. Even if the road is different from our expectations! However, if we quit at first sight of hardship, or if our belief fails us, we will never be able to achieve what we desire.

Labels

Everybody desires to do something, but they don't know how to complete the process of dedicating themselves and having the discipline to do it. If you have a desire, you gotta match that desire with your dedication and discipline.

What happens is a lot of people set these big goals, and look at them like a giant staircase that seems impossible to conquer. They start thinking that I can't, there's no way, it seems too difficult, that looks like too much work, and they never start.

Looking at the difficulty ahead, we start feeding our weaknesses by labeling ourselves incapable. Our unconscious mind makes us think it is easier to label ourselves incompetent than to work hard to attain our goals.

When we decide to get rid of addiction, our unconscious mind begins feeding us the idea that we are not strong enough to combat our addiction. We start thinking about when our addiction will get a hold of us. We will lose all the hard work put into those few days of our struggle against addiction. Our unconscious brain keeps on labeling us as the "loser." You will start thinking about all the times you decided something and ended up being a loser. Eventually, you will stop putting effort into your goals and see yourself as a loser.

Another form of "labels" also exists, and because of this notion, I deviate from the NA or AAs. When you are in NA or AA, you first have to share your story, and you start that story by labeling yourself. You start by saying, "Hi! I am an addict" or "I am an alcoholic." By saying all this, you label yourself an addict and keep repeating it until it gets etched into your unconscious mind.

So, when you decide to combat addiction, this label surfaces, saying you are an addict, you always have been, and this is your reality. No! This isn't true. You might have been addicted to something and had been an addict, but this is not your whole reality. You are more than that. You are more powerful than that. If you are not currently active, according to the meaning of the word addicted (unable to stop), if you have stopped and no longer depend on it, you are no longer an addict. It's time for a new label, a new belief.

Addiction is just a misaligned ray of life's energy. You still have a cosmos of powerful and positive energy inside you. Your past addiction has left a hole ready to be filled with magnetic energy.

So, stop saying you are an addict and start believing in yourself. It would help if you started repeating to yourself that you are nothing but positivity; you have the potential, the ability to be better, and the capability to be at the top of that staircase.

You gotta get past that thinking that you're not worthy. You have to get past the thought that you can't do it. You have to get past the labeling that you're an idiot, you're ugly, you're too fat, you're too skinny, and you've been hooked on to something all your life that you can't change. You must get past this thinking and start believing it's possible; I can do it. Because in the vortex, everything is possible.

Regret and Worry

Regret and worry, often known as the past and the future, are two of the most powerful and prevalent unpleasant emotions that impact our lives daily. Every waking minute, we are immersed in a stream of awareness. In our heads, one idea follows the next every second, and those thoughts primarily concern the past and the future.

The only significant moment is the one we pay the least attention to in the present. Everything takes place here. Everything you feel and see occurs in the now. That is all there is to life: a succession of current moments.

The past is just all of the current moments that have passed. The future is just a collection of all current moments that are yet to occur. As a result, life at any time other than the present is pointless – even if your ongoing work is directed toward the future.

Assume you have a paper due in two weeks. You might lament the time you didn't spend working on it, but that's pointless. Neither is concerned about the large amount of work yet to come. The most effective method to complete the task is to concentrate on what you can accomplish right now: Calm down, sit, think, identify the issue, create an outline, and begin preparing.

Life is a succession of present moments, and the only one you can truly savor is right now. However, your present can get plagued by the choices or events that happened in your past.

Pain and suffering greatly affect a person's life and belief system. These are the reasons for the development of limiting beliefs. Suffering and pain are the shackles that don't allow us to grow and live in the present moment.

Past and future are the main sources of suffering in one's life. We keep on regretting the decisions that we made in the past, and we keep on worrying about making the decisions that will affect our future. Our suffering arises in this realm between regret and worry.

We do not understand that we are the greatest source of our suffering. We are creating unnecessary pain for ourselves by remaining trapped in the future and the past without realizing the importance of the present. Our regret and worry prove that we cannot accept our present and enjoy it. Our mind is entangled in choices that have no existence at this point.

Past

Our minds are created in such a way that they like to create pain. They do this to make you abandon the present because it unconsciously perceives that you are not the best version of yourself. It keeps you from accepting your true self by producing pain and feeding on the past. Because the mind cannot operate and maintain control without time, which includes both the past and the future, it resists the timeless now.

Our mind feeds this resistance through our guilt—the guilt of things we have done in the past. The guilt of the decisions we make will seemingly make our future worse. You are more aware of the present than of the past. And it's possible that in the past, when you weren't aware, you did things you now recognize as wrong, or you caused misery to another person or beings. And you can see it now. You didn't realize what you were doing at the time because you weren't aware enough to behave differently. The fact that a person feels guilty now indicates that they can see something they could not see before. But now you realize you've awoken, and you might view a lot of your history as dysfunctional, unconscious behavior that caused you and others pain. Almost every unconscious person inflicts pain on himself and others without realizing it. They cause unhappiness and make others unhappy. That is what unconscious people do—some to a greater extent than others. As a result, guilt may arise as you awaken. And our mind keeps driving this guilt, making us lose belief in ourselves.

So how can the mind, which has great power, be defeated? The answer is acceptance. Accepting your true self is the only way to shatter the mind's resistance and snap out of your past. However, if remaining in the present moment was simple, most of us would do it all the time. Redirecting your attention to the present requires continual work. Two methods may be useful. Inquiring as to what your next thought will be. And observing, but not judging, your thoughts and desires.

Physics inspires the first method. Quantum particles are continually in motion. We can tell where or when they are, but never both simultaneously. The only way to keep such a complex system running is to monitor it. Only then will its features stay constant. This is referred to as the *Quantum Zeno effect.*

When it comes to mindfulness, asking oneself about future actions can postpone your next thought. It can also allow you to figure out how much time you spend on autopilot.

You're interrupting your thoughts to get away from them. You'll also choose each idea more carefully.

The second method is more traditional, "the Zen." It is a matter of listening and accepting without acting. Keep an eye out for nagging ideas like "I should have done it sooner," but don't let them take over your thinking. As they pass by, make a wave. Refrain from your mind's regretful and worried inclinations by noticing, seeing, and accepting the truth.

Separating your physical, observant body from your restless mind reduces the friction between the present, past, and future. Hence, the agony you feel over things can't be altered.

Quantum Zeno Effect and Future

The quantum Zeno effect arises from the classical Zeno paradox proposed by the Zeno of Elea. Let's assume that there is an arrow in motion. It will take a few seconds to reach its destination. However, if we observe this arrow at an instant in time, it will seem like it is not moving; it is motionless. So, if we split up those few seconds into multiple instances in time, then observing the arrow at all these instances will make it motionless. Hence, you can freeze an object by monitoring it again and again.

Let's try to understand this with a simpler example. Imagine that you are trying to watch a video on YouTube. You try to open it up, and the video starts loading. You observe that your internet is slow, and the video takes longer than expected. A thought comes into your mind; let's close your eyes and check the video periodically. This might work as time travel and speed up the video. However, according to the Zeno paradox, this idea of your time travel will freeze time. Whenever you open your eyes to observe the video, the loading will stop for that instant, and the more observations you make, the more motionless it becomes. Nothing appeared to change when you looked at the loading symbol! Because, according to the quantum Zeno effect, nothing or very little changed. You could stop the video's evolution (supposing that the video genuinely obeys quantum rules) by monitoring the video often enough at certain intervals.

The Zeno paradox might not apply to the world we see with our naked eye; however, the Zeno effect does occur in the quantum world. Suppose we start observing and measuring a radioactive, decaying particle in the quantum world. In that case, it will be observed that the decaying rate of that particle will slow down the more we observe it. So, if we can observe or measure it every instant, there will be no change in the measurements, and the particle will remain frozen.

Your brain is a powerful organ, processing multiple thoughts and emotions in a nick of a second. So when you keep stressing and thinking about what you will do next, the brain will keep observing your action every instance and freezing the time.

You might have felt this effect when you needed to make some important decision. When you start thinking about what to do or choose, you will observe that the time is slow. The more you think about it, the more motionless you become. However, the time reverts to the normal flow when you conclude, decide, and let go of the thought. Everything starts to feel in normal motion.

So, when you keep thinking about the future, your future won't grow or develop. It will remain frozen and won't allow your next thought, freezing your life. So, for your future to unfold in its actual potential, you need to stop being stressed and think about your future actions. Allow yourself to be on auto-pilot most of the time, and you will do just fine.

Visualization

Now that you know better how our beliefs can affect our journey against addiction. Let's talk about how to strengthen your belief in success. One of the most beneficial techniques that you can try is visualization.

Visualization is a mental practice that uses imagination to help us achieve our goals in life. Visualization can help us attain success and wealth and improves our lives when applied correctly. Our minds are powerful, and visualization uses our minds to achieve our desire.

Interestingly, people visualize every day but are unaware of it. Visualization is a similar process to daydreaming. For example, suppose someone has a strong desire to possess a magnificent home and visualizes it often. Thus, he will attract the house into his life. Although it may seem magical, visualization is only a natural process fueled by the power of thinking. Visualization works so that the subconscious mind interprets one's dominant ideas as instructions, which results in persistent and continuous attempts to emulate them through physical activity. The dominant concept is powerfully supported by burning desire, which leads one to devote all efforts to its fulfillment.

People achieve success through using the power of imagery, whether consciously or unconsciously. And so, the vision of the intended goal is critical to achieving it.

What Is the Function of Visualization and Why Does it Work?

Visualization focuses attention and strength on a single dominant notion. A thought has magnetic energy, which attracts other similar energies. Every event in our lives begins with a simple notion. We can observe this concept in action when, for example, someone constantly thinks about a friend and then meets that friend or receives a call or email from them. By having an imagination and consistently keeping it in our minds, we physically attract and generate that idea via visualization. You will invite disease if you continuously assume you are sick. If you believe you are happy, you will undoubtedly attract happiness. As a result, the deliberate vision of what we desire in life assists us in manifesting it. This is the capability of visualization.

It isn't easy to imagine the beach if you've never visited it. You won't get that whole sensory experience even viewing beach images online. The fragrance of the sea and the taste of salt, the warm sun on your toes, and the cold frothy white water swirling around your ankles, their imagination, needs prior experience.

Similarly, becoming something that we cannot envision is difficult. As a result, we must practice envisioning. This is how visualizing comes into play.

Quantum Side of Visualization

The Science of visualization extends beyond Classical Physics, which deals with things and forces we see and touch daily. Newton's three principles of motion are well-known to us, and their portrayal in our environment makes perfect sense to us.

However, there is a more fundamental representation in Quantum Reality, which we cannot see or comprehend with our five senses. Quantum physics is concerned with another reality that permeates everything but is buried out of our sight.

This means that the cosmos around us is alive with endless options until we select and choose one of them. Only when we, as observers, make that choice does the cosmos reflect that choice as our reality among the innumerable other possibilities.

Sometimes in history, scientists found that all subatomic particles have both the properties of waves and particles. The path to this revelation is very interesting. Thomas Young experimented with investigating the behavior of light. The double-slit experiment expected that light would behave like a wave.

When the experiment was set up to detect light, it produced an interference pattern representing a wave property. The major shock came when the experiment was slightly changed. It was assumed that light is formed of particles, and detectors were fitted to observe the direction the photons of light particles took.

What type of trend would we see now? We see two small spots of light. Why? We identified particles because we thought of light as particles, and particles cannot interfere with each other like waves.

When we experiment, assuming that light is a particle, light acts as if it were formed of particles. However, experimenting with the assumption that light is a wave will result in light behaving as if it were a wave.

The experiment clearly shows that what we see is what our universe contains. The cosmos only gives us the side of itself that we choose to see. Our world is only a mirror of our inner ideas, beliefs, and attitudes. We genuinely feel what we picture when we practice visualization meditation. According to quantum physics, our reality is defined by what we experience. As a result, what we imagine becomes a reality in our world.

Visualization and Addiction

The question of how to use visualization to stand a chance against addiction. You can do this by visualizing yourself as the winner. You have to practice seeing yourselves at the finish line; practice seeing yourselves winning the trophy. Imagine yourself living away from the depths of addiction in a healthy and peaceful environment. Whenever you are faced with a self-limiting belief or label, visualize the opposite. Imagine the positive side and keep feeding the winner inside you.

People who get sober will have to rebuild their lives. It may seem frightening at first, but there are some distinct benefits to being able to restart. Once you have established a solid foundation in recovery, you will be ready to begin constructing the sort of life you want. Positive visualizations can be beneficial in helping you to progress on the right path.

Visualization will not only keep you motivated but will also help you to build a deeper understanding of what you want to accomplish. If you believe in these mental representations, you are already halfway to your ultimate objective.

§

Mental Contrasting

From what you have read, you might think that visualization only involves thinking about the positive outcomes. However, this is not the case. You will achieve the best results when you visualize the positive and negative aspects at the same time. This concept might feel a bit confusing now, but keep reading about the mental contrasting, and you will know precisely what visualizing the negative aspects means.

Mental contrasting is the act of imagining your intended objectives as well as the potential internalimpediments that may prevent you from accomplishing your goals.

Mental contrasting is a technique for recognizing the distance between where you are now and where you wish to go. It also helps you to feel the discomfort or tension that comes with that gap. Mental contrasting is a much more realistic mode of thought. It is more than just optimistic thinking. It is also not limited to negative thoughts. Mental contrasting is a practical approach to considering where you concern your objectives.

To be successful, you must do both steps: practice positive visualization to enhance your confidence that you will be able to accomplish your objective and create high expectations for yourself. And you must use negative visualization to see and control any obstacles along the way.

Suppose you are aware of the hurdles and believe that you have a high possibility of overcoming them. In that case, you will be inspired and invigorated to take action. Conversely, if you doubt that you will overcome the barriers, you will become less driven and begin to postpone. This is why your objectives must be achievable. It's difficult but not impossible.

The process of mental contrasting will leave you with the impression that you will succeed and the feeling that it will be difficult. There are several challenges that you must be aware of and address. But the journey does not end there!

Of course, practicing mental contrasting just once is preferable to doing no mental contrasting at all. However, it would be best if you practiced contrasting mental daily to benefit from this process fully. A new belief does not emerge overnight. The subconscious mind requires repetition. Furthermore, you will progress toward your objectives every day. This implies that daily mental contrasting will give you fresh insights into new barriers associated with the new you or challenges you have never considered.

Discover

The first significant advantage of mental contrasting is that it will assist you in discovering how your existing self does not match your future aspirations. Therefore, mental contrast is an excellent way to reflect on yourself, where you are, and what you need to work on next.

Mental contrasting creates significant, subconscious links between the difficulties you see and the solutions you apply. And so, it helps you explore your mentality and manner of thinking. You may utilize this to your advantage to choose which measures to take. This might include taking concrete steps toward your goal, but it can also involve changing negative ideas into positive ones.

Handling Negative Feedback

You will be able to handle unfavorable comments if you use mental contrasting. Negative feedback is all around us. This is a completely natural occurrence. No matter how amazing your last presentation was, there will always be a tiny proportion of individuals who disagree with you. Instead of allowing negative criticism to defeat you, you should learn to deal with it productively.

Mental contrasting is an excellent method for coping with this negative feedback. It teaches you how to cope with problems successfully and constructively and that erroneous feedback is another impediment. Dealing with challenges becomes a habit due to mental contrasting, and you gain self-esteem since you know you can emerge victorious.

Mental Contrasting Against Addiction

To use mental contrasting effectively for combating addiction, you need to focus more on positive visualization. First, you will visualize yourself as a winner, filling yourself with positivity and experiencing the feeling of being free from the shackles.

Once you master this, you will start using the contrasting mental technique. As you continue to visualize and think about the potential obstacles you might face on your journey, the positive effects will keep neutralizing them. Mental contrasting will help you identify the challenges, and then you can work on yourself and improve. You will visualize overcoming those obstacles that will come your way.

You will eventually reach a point when you cannot find any significant barriers. This is when you must leap in faith and be free from the shackles of addiction.

You might be wondering why I started my book with such difficult concepts. The answer is "necessity." The mind is very powerful. It can work as a powerful creation lab and the most secure prison. Addiction has locked us into this mind prison. Therefore, we needed to break free from it before we began the journey toward a healthy and prosperous life.

So, try to learn from this chapter as much as you can before moving on. You can read the chapter over or focus on the summary to review what you have learned. Let's work together to bring an end to addiction.

Summary

Addiction is not a character flaw or a sign of weakness; it takes more than determination to overcome it. Confidence and belief that you can overcome addiction are the hardest to sustain. We are less likely to act, alter, or strive to improve circumstances when we lack self-confidence and belief. Therefore, believing in ourselves can support, empower, and guide us toward our ultimate goal.

The Law of Belief states that whatever you believe with passion and conviction becomes your reality. You can't change your reality unless you change your beliefs. For example, all of the world's religions highlight the ability to maintain faith as a key to happiness and wealth. Therefore, the trick is to have total clarity on your objectives and an outstanding plan for achieving them.

Desire is natural for everyone, but devotion is where everyone struggles. They don't know how to devote themselves to it and maintain the discipline to do it. Our unconscious mind convinces us that labeling oneself inept is simpler than working hard to achieve our objectives. When we desire to overcome our addiction, our unconscious mind begins to convince us that we are not strong enough to overcome it. However, this is far from true. Addiction is a misplaced ray of your vital force, and you have a plethora of positive energy to balance it.

When you feel you have a good chance of overcoming addiction, you will be motivated to take action. Conversely, if you question your ability to conquer the obstacles, you will become less motivated and continue to postpone. So, stop labeling yourself and start believing in your power.

My Story

In another one of America's crazy ghettos, another ordinary, typical horror story product of the environment, a black man was made from the creation of two hard-working, middle-class black parents. The early stages of my life were formed from a combination of older family members, my cousins, and peers from my environment, so it was no surprise crime, drugs, and prison were in my future. At the age of 15, I had begun selling heroin; by 19, it had elevated to crack and cocaine. My older cousins around me were already dipping and dabbing with drug use. My brother was an original gangster with severe heroin addiction and was murdered in an alley in one of Baltimore's worse hoods.

By my twenties, I led a band of 15 or more thugs with over 20 guns. We began to rob, steal, shoot, and cause harm and havoc to anyone we felt would assist on our road to riches. My first prison sentence was at 23 at the Baltimore penitentiary for a handgun violation, where I was reunited with a slightly older cousin. Soon after, my crime spree elevated to white-collar crimes full time, from being schooled by another older cousin just coming home from a manslaughter sentence and only blazing robberies if the stakes were high enough to spark my interest.

Not long after my crime spree with white collar began, I was caught in the crossfire and appeared on the news for a robbery.

Shortly after, I was convicted and sentenced to three concurrent 15-year sentences for a home invasion.

Not the home invasion that occurred, but one that I was completely innocent of. The victim showed up in court, pointed at me, and said, I'll never forget your face. I had never seen this man a day in my life.

I valued my time in prison, knowing I was innocent of the crime I was accused of and being a spiritual man. I took this brief time to develop as a man. I began to study religion as a whole. Having a good relationship with the all-white captains and majors in the prison, I was able to have my request answered immediately, which was nothing but requesting family members and those able to teach me lessons as cell buddies.

I began regularly receiving lessons from Muslims, Israelites, Morris Americans, and Christians. Also, due to an older cousin deeply caught up in the life of drugs and deception and me being a younger cousin, 270lbs able to lift anything in the yard pit or prison as a whole with a feared reputation and a menacing presence, which is a big no-no.

Later it led to my nephew and me as cell buddies, who were older than me, by years and had the same name {rip Lil Joe}, but was overlooked. It was the prison that gave me the discipline to make the change. I needed to be still yet active in a recovery program. My recovery program. It was the prison where I discovered my speaking talent; having a stuttering problem was not something I was expecting. My message was powerful and deadly on point.

I was elected to be the speaker for black history month. Where I spoke for 30 minutes in front of at least 5000 inmates. My title was WAKE UP. It was a cold, rude awakening speech from this big strong inmate who rarely even talked. It was one of 6 other speeches I wrote in a day. I was focused.

I kept my good energy when I returned from prison after 5 years. However, I wasn't living on purpose, which was speaking. I had some houses that I had purchased before being sentenced. I sold one and got a crooked loan for another for 80 grand. Altogether, I had about $100,000.

The same office I got my loan from gave me a $220,000 line of credit. I purchased a seven-room, 2-unit Duplex.

A two-unit, seven-room Duplex. Unfortunately, my mind was still focused on the streets. So what did I do? I purchased a kilo of cocaine. For a short while, life was one big party.

Eating oysters, shots of Stolis, and lines of coke. Not long after, one of my partners got 25 years with the feds, and my other got hooked on crack. During this time, I met a beautiful young lady while leaving the gym on my daily workout routine with my partner, who was going through a divorce. That year, her husband made $40 million. She was rolling in the dough.

For my birthday, she dropped $150,000 in shoes, clothes, coats, jewelry, and cologne. I had been upgraded and felt a major shift in my being for the first time. Then my mom died, and life took a drastic turn for the worst. Being the only child of Joe and Thelma, I felt like I was always in the spotlight; I was Joe Frank, the family's prince. I had the prettiest women, always had nice clothes and cars, and an image of THE MAN I had to uphold. When mom died, it felt like I deserved a well-needed rest and grounds to FUCK UP.

I decided to step up my drug use. I took my first hit of crack. You see, I used to give advice all the time. I thought it was easy to stop getting high.

Whoever I advised would always ask me one question had I ever gotten high before? Had I ever smoked, cracked, or sniffed heroin? And my answer was always no. And all my advice was null and void. No matter how loud I shouted or how many times I said it, no one listened.

So I said, okay, I'm going to show these fools I can beat this addiction like a pro. Well, one month led to two, and three led to four. One year led to five. Five years led to ten.

Remember the seven-room, two-unit duplex? Well, before I lost it, it turned into a hotel crack whore. I was the known crack whore pimp with the best girls. My house was a never-ending revolving door of whores and tricks. Wild nights, porno, drug fights, and ducking cops and bounty hunters. Remember the rich girlfriend? Well, she left me after several attempts to make it right. Remember all the clothes? Every hustler within 25 miles had Gucci belts, Louis shoes, Prada belts, tailor-made suits, diamond watches, et cetera.

Things quickly spiraled downhill between me beating, shooting, and stabbing irate tricks. Being a block bully got me shot up close range 3 times. I was so high I didn't feel a thing besides a drop of blood on my shirt; you couldn't even tell I had been shot. So I didn't bother going to the hospital. Besides, one of my girls had money and drugs, so I had more important things to do.

Not long after, my bottom bitch got pregnant and had a baby. It was a miracle we brought the baby home from the hospital... To a seven-room, two-unit, three-bathroom, run-down and abandoned, that I owned—nothing working in the middle of summer, no AC, no shower, no toilet. Just my flies and a newborn baby cause the mother was out chasing drugs all day and night and tricking from sun up till sundown. But now it's almost a year in foreclosure with no running water or electricity. About a month later, CPS stepped in for a long court battle that resulted in the baby being placed in foster care and eventually adopted out. I had had enough of Baltimore and decided to pack up and move to New York.

But as Grandma said, you will still be there no matter where you go. I cleaned up long enough to make a good impression on my daughter. Thanks to my daughter's Mom and best friend.

Soon after, I moved to the Bronx, and all hell broke loose. I became a monster. Running through the projects, beating up junkies, stealing and getting high all day and night, running like a chicken with his head cut off. That's when I got stabbed by a three-foot midget I had beaten up before for threatening me. The stab was pretty bad enough to snap me out of my habit and wake me up in a big way.

In a big way, he did me a huge favor. My dad was suffering from dementia and doing badly, so I decided to move back to Baltimore. So I packed up and headed home. But now I was homeless, living out of the truck that I managed to buy from some cash I put together from some scams I ran.

However, living on the streets of Baltimore was different than in New York. It wasn't safe, making it hard to sleep at night. And besides, I couldn't drive around all day with no license like in New York, so I had to limit my driving. So I decided to pick up one of my old habits, my good old friend heroine.

Or. Now, by this time, Fentanyl. That made it easier to find a good parking spot, smoke a cigarette, sniff some blow and fall out until the next day. It didn't take long before I passed out behind the wheel and crashed into four cars with women and children as passengers; I woke up to the cops shoving Narcan up my nose and being arrested for about 15 charges. I was shortly released and got a job at a car wash in my old neighborhood by my karate sensa during the day. By talking to the mailman, I found an abandoned house with all the furniture, TV, and electricity still on but no running water. The first night in, I was spotted breaking in, and the cops were called, but I remained still and quiet until they left; for the next few weeks, this was my home. That lasted about a month or so.

And something inside of me said, look at you. Look at your life. You're living in an abandoned house, working at a car wash, not raising my kids, not being productive, and most of all, not living on purpose.

That was it. I had had enough. We all have different rock bottoms, but this was mine. I've left out a lot, trust me, it was all hell and high water. I checked myself into a treatment program and made it up in my mind. I was done wasting time. I was done spinning my wheels.

I was done being a deadbeat. I was done not being the person I believed I knew I was meant to be. That's when I started to align myself. And stepped into what I call THE VORTEX.

That's when I decided I would get connected to the universe and let lose my inner game, my inner gain. And at that second, life changed.
I learned to meditate. I still haven't mastered it. I learned to focus on my goal by concentrating on one or two words simultaneously. My two words are love and abundance. First, love.

Everybody needs love. Love makes the heart grow fonder. First, you must be lovable and open to love if you want to love. Smile has a pleasant attitude; be warm inside regardless of your surroundings—lastly, abundance.

We are here on this Earth to achieve things, to be creators, and to manifest great things. This is how we activate the law of abundance to the fullest. This is how we align with purpose and power. This is how we activate our inner gain. There's a magnet in us all that attracts forces in the universe that sends us exactly what we deserve, what we focus on the most, what we truly believe we are worthy of.

Nothing happens by coincidence. You get what you give out. Learn to vibrate on higher frequencies. Learn where to apply your focus. Exercise. Smile. Ask yourself:

How much time do I want to waste? We don't lose in life because we don't have talent. We lose in life because we're not in our position. So as I began to align myself with my purpose, I began to shift in position. I wanted love desperately.

I was missing something in life, a partner. So one day, I received a phone call, a phone message from a dating app, and said, I'm not stalking you, but we met years ago on the train in Harlem. By any chance, is your last name Stokes? My name is Candice, and I'm a love coach and hypnotherapist. We met on the train one day about six yearsvago.

And you gave me your card. I lost it since then, and it's been a long time, but in the words of Candace, this was the divine right timing. The double Dutch game of life is always being played. The ropes are always spinning. The key is to get in the rhythm so you can jump in

Next is manifesting abundance, which, once aligned properly, never stops. I had already started building content and getting ready for the opportunity to present itself, which was essential. Please don't wait for the chance to get ready; get ready for the chance when we get ready; the universe brings the chance to our door. That's when I got my first speaking engagement. I remember that accident where I crashed in the back of 4 people and was arrested. Well, it was dismissed. I began to make YouTube videos from my room in a recovery house. The Quantum Side of Addiction. I returned to court for my license, where at least 20 charges were dismissed. I received my license back, and the rest is history. It's all possible if you first believe and know it is. These are the keys to opening the VORTEX.

Laws and Principles

Everything in our cosmos is significantly more intelligent than we give it credit for. Our lives are ruled by stunning coherence. The more we quit trying to control the result and go with the flow, the more magic will be manifested. Our cosmos loves absolute, ubiquitous, consistent, and neutral laws and principles. We may claim ignorance of the complicated workings of these rules. But, whether we are conscious of it or not, we are constantly engaging with and using these principles in our lives.

Subconsciously, we all know these divine laws of the universe. These principles and laws are the backbones of the universe's working body. This chapter will teach us about the universe's laws to understand its complexity.

Laws of the universe are essential because they bring nature into balance and harmony. You will better understand how the universe operates if you learn these laws. Once you've learned the rules, you can apply them to your personal life to advance prosperity. Every universal rule is a piece of the complicated jigsaw that is the universe. They are all linked and operate together. As such, they can be a guide for making the most of life. Let's take a closer look at the universal laws, how they affect our life, and how you may use them to your advantage..

The Hermetic Principles

Everyone wants to know how the world works, where people fit in, and how we can use our understanding of the two to live happier and more fulfilling lives. For this purpose, philosophers strove to comprehend the cosmos and natural law thousands of years ago. They authored various old philosophical texts in search of a complete guide to the world's rules. These manifestations have been written down and published in the Kybalion manuscript. The Kybalion comprises hermetic teachings that outline the seven natural laws and the universe's principles. These seven principles form the basis of Hermeticism, a spiritual philosophy that dates back to the first century A.D. They were written by renowned author Hermes Trismegistus, credited with writing the Emerald Tablet and the Corpus Hermeticum.

The Principle of Mentalism

Everything in the cosmos is, first and foremost, a mental construct. As described previously, quantum physics has proved this law of the universe through the concept of electrons showing the properties of waves and particles. This implies that you must first have a concept for something before creating it. On the most evident level, this occurs whenever an idea becomes a concrete object via the inspired action of another person.

However, on a deeper level, your thoughts and ideas might arouse cravings for specific experiences or "things" in your life. So if your thoughts are filled with anxiety and dread because of concern, your life experiences will prove that your beliefs are real and well-founded. However, your experiences will be positive if you approach life with love and inner serenity.

This is why it looks as though the rich become wealthier while the poor get poorer. Since the rich are constantly focused on plenty and live in it, it is much easier for them to adopt a prosperous mentality. On the other hand, those who live in poverty are continuously confronted with financial difficulties, stress, and feelings of scarcity, all of which exacerbate an already dire situation. However, we can change our life experiences by changing our thoughts.

Everything in this universe is here to assist us in achieving what we imagine and desire. Starting with the belief that we are powerful enough to combat addiction and win over it will harmonize our life energy with the universe's energy. And the universe will make our imagination come true.

However, this doesn't mean you can achieve anything without hard work. Our beliefs and imagination will create a mindset and drive us to work hard to achieve what we truly desire.

The Mind

The quantum side of every reality and matter present in this universe starts from the mind. This principle does not specifically refer to the brain as the mind. It is a set of organs ranging from the heart to the gut to several parts of the brain, which combine to make us our reality. Our whole body can work as our mind. When all the energies of our body become balanced and work in harmony, that is when we achieve our true form, and the power of our mind gets amplified.

To understand the concept of harmony more clearly, we need to know more about our brains. The brain has many parts, but three main parts are the brain stem, cerebellum, and cerebral cortex. The cerebral cortex is further divided into the frontal lobe, temporal lobe, parietal lobe, and occipital lobe. A detailed description of all these parts is out of the scope of this book. Nevertheless, their functions demonstrate the cohesive bodywork of all these parts, leading to harmony.

The brain stem serves as a relay center and transmits information. Moreover, it regulates heart rate, breathing rate, and balance. Sudden injuries and other heart and brain conditions can affect its performance.

The cerebellum involves motor learning, balance and equilibrium, body positioning, and movement coordination. It performs these actions with the assistance of the vestibular system. So, any damage to the vestibular system will affect its working.

The frontal lobes are vital for expressive language, regulating higher-level executive functions and voluntary movement. The temporal lobes play a role in processing emotions, language, and certain elements of visual perception. Senses such as taste, hearing, and sight rely on the parietal lobe for processing and integration. The occipital lobe is responsible for visual processing. Memory formation and face recognition are all aided by this brain function, as are spatial processing, depth perception, color identification, and visual perception.

All these functions of the cerebral cortex result from processing information sent to the brain from other organs. So, any issue with any of the body's organs can affect the brain and, consequently, the processing of vital information. Hence, for optimum body functioning, all the organs need to be in harmony with each other.

Your body becomes a singularity filled with unending energy when this harmony is achieved. It becomes the mind, and the imagination or thought forming in your mind is relayed to the body. The whole body amplifies the energy of that thought, ultimately bringing it to reality.

Therefore, to strengthen ourselves against addiction, we need to bring harmony to our whole body, transforming it into a singular mind and imagining ourselves free of addiction.

The Principle of Vibration

Everything in the cosmos vibrates at a certain frequency. Therefore, you must match that frequency to what you desire to make anything appear. A high-powered microscope can reveal that matter is nothing more than space, with a few specks of energy sprinkled here and there. A person's body is composed of molecules, which indicates that we're nothing more than energy bundles. Exquisitely well-structured and polished, yet lacking in everything else. You can't see or conceive of anything except energy. It's well-ordered and intricate, but it's energy.

The table is considerably harder than your hand, which begs the question: if everything is formed of energy, why is that? What's the difference if they're both created of energy? Their vibration is what distinguishes them. There are various frequencies and speeds of vibration in the energy of everything. Please take a closer look at water in all three of its varieties. In ice, water molecules move slowly, while in liquid, they move quickly. Molecules split and become airborne as water converts to steam due to their rapid vibratory motion.

While your body and everything you identify as "you" has a unique vibration, your thoughts, which you create, also have unique vibrations that alter or blend with your total vibratory frequency.

Vibrations are sent from you to everyone and everything you come into contact with - from the people and animals around you to the inanimate things and even space. Because of this, when you enter a room where there was a previous altercation, you can smell it. The tension in the room is so intense that we characterize it as having bad vibrations.

You're constantly vibrating in the world around you. The vibrations of everything and everyone around you are also being received and translated by you simultaneously. Think of yourself as both a television transmitter and receiver. You can tune in to all the stations and frequencies aired around you, just as a television transmitter beams out its unique channel.

The Quantum Side

Everything is energy in quantum physics, according to the concept of vibration. There are only two types of vibrations, namely, positive and negative. You emit a vibration, whether it's a good or bad one, whenever you feel anything.

When you think negatively, you send a frequency into the cosmos, which returns to its source; therefore, whatever you feel like returning to you is a bad idea. Therefore, taking care of the quality of your ideas and learning how to generate more pleasant ones is essential.

When you watch movies or television shows about tragedies like death or betrayal, your brain interprets this as fact. It sends a cascade of chemicals into your system, altering your natural vibrational frequency. Similarly, your vibrational frequency will suffer if you spend much time in a filthy or disorganized setting.

Helping With Addiction

To attain a happy life without addiction, we must fill ourselves with positive vibrations and make our energy oscillate with our thoughts of having a beautiful and happy life. Producing positive thoughts, surrounding ourselves with positive people, looking and experiencing positive things, and keeping the environment free of negative energy will amplify your positive vibration. These positive vibrations will align with your desires and bring them to life. In short, keep your vibrations positive and eliminate the addiction, manifesting a happy life.

The Principle of Correspondence

According to the Law of Correspondence, there is always a correspondence between the outside and inner worlds - "as inside, so without" or "as above, so below." There is a connection between what happens around us and within us. In other words, our external environment reflects our inner world. This indicates that if our inner world is unpleasant, so will our external environment. If we have poor self-esteem, feel horrible about ourselves, or are continually filled with rage, hate, or loathing, our outer world will be miserable, chaotic, or unfulfilling, acting as a direct reflection of what is happening inside us.

Thoughts and pictures in our awareness manifest unconsciously in our exterior surroundings. The mind accepts everything as it is and starts to replicate precisely what we focus on, good or terrible. It makes no difference what we attempt to alter on the outside if we don't also try to change it on the inside. Our world will continue to take on the characteristics of our inner state.

A garden can be used to illustrate the rule of correspondence. This garden is in your thoughts. As you pick weeds from your garden, you must also eliminate weeds from your thoughts and nourish the soil with fruitful things. As you gain this understanding, you will continuously look inside to develop yourself and attract your aspirations.

The Quantum side

In quantum physics, there is a principle of correspondence that implies that for any new theory to arise, it must be reduced to the previously proven theories. This means that every new theory and change acts as outside behavior and directly relates to what is already inside (already proven theories). Through this principle, physics states that no external thing can deviate from what is inside. Unless the already proven theories (inside) are not changed, we can't prove any deviating theory.

Helping With Addiction

The Law of Correspondence wants you to remember that unless you begin paying attention to what's inside, you will be trapped in a victim mindset, creating a world that does not benefit you. You will not alter your reality unless you learn the lessons. As a result, now is the moment to be mindful of your inner world and whatever you do at the micro level since it will affect the macro level.

To eliminate addiction, we need to change ourselves from the inside. We must change our diets and how we cultivate our gardens. As soon as we change ourselves from the inside, we will automatically feel the addiction getting away from us.

The Principle of Polarity

Everything exists as a pair of opposites in this universe. Everything is dual and has poles. These poles are the same, but they vary in degree. The opposite extremes collide, resolving paradoxes and revealing that all truths are just half-truths.

This notion of polarity demonstrates that spirit and matter are only different speeds of vibration of the same substance. The All and the Many are seen to be the same among hermetic, with the distinction being varying degrees of mental expression.

According to the Law of Polarity, everything has its opposite. Only because pleasure exists does pain exist. Only because grief exists does happiness exist. Only because terrible times exist, good times exist. When something awful occurs, the Law of Polarity suggests that there is something good inside that evil. That is, all of these unpleasant and challenging situations are really for our benefit. Or, at the very least, we may make them that way by focusing on their positive aspects.

The polarity principle provides a clear picture of how transmutation works. Transmutation is altering the degree of the same item rather than changing it. For example, fear cannot be transformed into love. Still, it can be transformed into courage, just as hatred can be transformed into love.

The Quantum Side

Quantum physics was created to understand the concept of polarity. Scientists discovered that it existed in two places simultaneously when scientists examined the electron. Moreover, the electron showed the properties of a particle at one instance, while in other instances, it behaved like a wave.

And so, the concept of quantum polarity was formed to understand this phenomenon. Quantum polarity provides a new way of seeing and working with this world, making us aware of what is causing and supporting our problems. The concept of quantum polarity is that to understand the polarity of things; we must discover and understand the source causing the event. The duality of electrons was also understood by discovering their power source. It was revealed that the electron's energy is accumulated at a point, just like a particle. Thus, while the electron moves like a wave, it comes into contact with the matter at a single point, like a particle.

Helping With Addiction

In the case of fighting addiction, this principle of polarity can be of great help. We need to understand that every bad happening has some good hidden in it. What we need to do is change our view of things.

For example, instead of thinking of a car crash solely as a negative happening, we need to delve into the part in which this car crash can be used to identify the shortcomings and mistakes of the driver or the road.

Similarly, we need to change our view of addiction. We need to re-evaluate past traumas into present lessons of not failing but the lessons we learned from experience. This will allow us to heal from within and eliminate the source of our problem. Seeing the polar side of addiction will help us to get out of addiction and eliminate our shortcomings once and for all.

The Principle of Rhythm

Rhythm exists between opposing polarities, so anything at one extreme swing into the other equally. Every action has an equal and opposite response, like a pendulum swinging back and forth.

It is up to us to steady our wobble and preserve a feeling of inner peace and harmony regardless of our external circumstances since we will most likely see various ups and downs throughout our lives.

Because everything is energy first, emotions are the energy we feed to the individual that lives within. It only makes sense to stabilize our emotional state before stabilizing our physical experiences.

The rhythmic principle provides a window through which we may monitor and observe changes in our mental states. This principle adapts us to achieve more balance and peace of mind. Understanding the idea of rhythm teaches us to recognize and accept that all anguish and agony, like its opposites, pleasure, and happiness, are only transient.

Our rhythmic principle reveals that this stage of addiction is only transitory and will eventually be wiped out by the natural rhythm.

When we learn to harness this principle, we become more capable of elevating our vibrations, breaking behavioral patterns, and being more equipped to face the rising and falling waves in our lives. We can gain insight and self-awareness by applying this rhythmic concept to every circumstance, no matter how favorable or unpleasant. Knowing that this stage of addiction will not endure forever allows us to elevate our vibrations to materialize an addiction-free existence.

The Quantum Side

Everything in the cosmos can be broken down into particles or waves, which vibrate like strings at various frequencies. According to quantum scientists, everything in the cosmos is constantly vibrating. When particles resonate with one another, it creates a front that is unified and significant. This vibration creates an everlasting rhythm. This rhythm implies that every atom moves in a rhythmic cycle and will never remain in a permanent state. It will keep on moving and decaying because of the rhythm. The integrity of the matter depends on maintaining this rhythm.

Helping With Addiction

The law of rhythm tells us that nothing is permanent, everything is in a rhythm, and one day it will change. As discussed in the previous chapter, our subconscious mind creates certain labels for ourselves, imprinting on our minds that we won't be able to get out of addiction. The law of rhythm helps us to devour these labels.

When you need some hope that things will not always be how they are, this law will assist you in anticipating that your circumstances will change. This law tells us that this phase of addiction is just the absence of a higher self, and we can move the cycle of rhythm and bring it back. Laws such as this give us the self-confidence to change and move our addictions into the past.

§

The Principle of Cause and Effect

According to this principle, every cause has an effect, and every effect becomes the cause of something else. This rule implies that the cosmos is constantly in motion and advancing via a series of events. According to the Law, there are no accidents in this world, and the results we make in our life are a direct outcome of causes that originate inside ourselves.

Every single impact in our world, every single effect on our planet, has a source, an initial beginning place. All roads begin with an initial first step. From that first step, a chain reaction of events occur, with other offshoots extending in all directions. So, duplication and replication occur.

According to the law of cause and effect, all of your ideas, human behavior, and emotions impact the cosmos. Nothing in the cosmos is absolute, and everything is relative. As a result, when you move your hand, you move the space that surrounds it, which is linked to all space in the infinite cosmos. As a result, all inanimate items in the cosmos are linked from the inside and inhabit the same space or mind. There is no distinction. So, when you move your hand, you move the space connecting all things. Although it may take some time for some individuals to get their heads around the notion or concept, it is accurate. Everything in the cosmos has always existed in one form or another, that is, in its chemical or microscopic form, and everything arises from this.

The human mind causes movement, no matter how little, unless you actively remain motionless. All thoughts lead to actions or human behavior, and all actions and behavior lead to more thoughts. Every action is the product of thinking. A movement or action cannot occur without its original or previous thinking.

We are all guided by a chain reaction of events that begin with a cause. We are all bound by the universal rule of cause and effect.

The Quantum Side

In classical physics, there is a concept that a cause will bring about an effect, but the effect cannot become the cause. However, quantum physics deviates from it. In quantum physics, the cause can bring about an effect, and this effect can become the exact cause that brought it.

Taking alcohol as an example, consumption of alcohol (cause) brought about addiction (effect). When a person becomes addicted, he keeps on drinking alcohol. Alcohol was the cause of the addiction at the beginning of this case. Then addiction became the cause of drinking alcohol. Hence, the cause can bring about the effect, and the effect can bring about the exact cause.

Helping With Addiction

This law of the Universe can be used to help us on our journey against addiction as well. We need to understand that we will have to take the first step, which will act as the cause, and then the cycle will start, helping us to keep moving forward. When we start taking measures against addiction, the Universe will start to help us attain our goals. Staying away from alcohol will reduce addiction, and reduction of addiction will help us to stay away from liquor. Because we are connected to the Universe, bringing forth a cause to overcome addiction will be sensed by the entire Universe, and it will assist us in getting rid of our addiction.

Another lesson we need to get from the law of cause and effect is that only we are the cause of addiction. Our minds and deeds are the cause that brought the addiction, so only we have the power to reverse it. As a cause can create an effect, it also has the power to reverse it. Finding the cause of the addiction deep inside ourselves is the only way to reverse its effect.

The Principle of Gender

Gender is everywhere. Everything has Masculine and Feminine characteristics, and Gender emerges in all realms. Gender is derived from the Latin word beget, meaning procreate, generate, create, or produce.

In hermeticism, Gender does not relate to a person's physical sex or male or female reproductive organs. Gender presents itself differently in higher dimensions. Gender in hermeticism enables us to comprehend and see the action of both male and feminine energies interacting to generate all things in existence.

Masculine energy is defined in hermetic as penetrative, aggressive, progressive, conquesting, and actively channeling innate energy toward its feminine counterpart. Whereas feminine energy is responsive, holy, valued, protective, a keeper of traditions, upholding priority, and nurturing what is most important in life.

The male is associated with volition, while the feminine is associated with absorbing impressions from the masculine and developing new thoughts, concepts, and ideas, including imaginative activity.

The masculine will act without constraint, order, or reason in the absence of the feminine, ending in anarchy. Similarly, without the masculine, the feminine would endlessly reflect and fail to act, resulting in stagnation and lethargy. However, when the masculine and feminine energies mix, we witness purposeful action, the strength of the will and vision, the creative energy, and careful consideration to bring it to fruition.

The Quantum Side

As a particle in quantum reality, an electron cannot be torn apart and retain its identity when it collides with another particle. As a wave, it sweeps over huge swaths of space, is infinitely divisible, and integrates with other waves it encounters.

In general, males are particles, and women are waves. Men have an individual particle nature: a hard-shelled ego that is highly identifiable, a manly desire to keep competing identities in "collisions," and a drive to extreme behavior. Women, on the other hand, prefer to "merge" with groups in a collective wave. Now, let's look at alternating properties. Males are particle nature, but sometimes they become wave nature, caring, receiving, and nurturing. In the same way, even though females are wave natures, they can often become particle natures, aggressive and progressive.

Helping With Addiction

The important question here is how we can use this principle of gender against addiction. The main concept behind this principle is that you need to accept every part of yourself; your aggressive and progressive part and your soft and nurturing nature.

You might find yourself weak accepting both parts of yourself. Still, these counterparts working in conjunction with each other make you strong. This is the middle path; it is all about balancing the masculine and feminine, the divine and the earthbound, and the mind, body, and soul. When we reach this internal equilibrium, we are well prepared to harness all of the principles mentioned earlier and apply them to our war against addiction. Accept your masculinity and femininity and become ready to fight addiction as your whole self.

Law of Attraction

The Law of Attraction employs the power of the mind to transfer whatever is in our minds into reality. The fundamental definition of the Law of Attraction is that like attracts like, and all ideas eventually materialize into things.

If you dwell on the bad, you will remain in that cloud. If you think positively and set objectives for yourself, you will find a way to attain them via fruitful actions. This is why the Universe is so breathtakingly lovely.

According to the Law of Attraction, anything that can be envisioned and kept in the mind's eye is attainable if you take action to reach where you want to go. The only thing that you need is imagination and the belief that you can attain what you desire. This attitude will trigger the power of the mind, transforming your desire or imagination into reality.

The Quantum Side and Role in Addiction

All energy particles in the cosmos are entangled, and a field surrounds all energy particles with infinite potential for location, form, and behavior. The observer effect is a well-known phenomenon in quantum physics. It states that by observing a particle, we can change its behavior. Putting the observer effect in practical life implies that observing, focusing, and providing attention to what is not yet existent in your life quickly brings it to reality. The observer's thought determines where what, and how energy manifests. You are an observer in your own life. Observing ourselves and focusing our energy on the manifestation of a better future self will bring about the observer effect. Our energy will bring our imagination of life without addiction to reality.

Law of Relativity

Nobody or nothing is intrinsically good or terrible. Everything is a spectrum of expression, and every event or difficulty has several perspectives. In other words, we are the ones who attach meaning to events. Therefore, we may choose to see things negatively or positively. Having a positive attitude along the journey toward change is very important because positive energy is the one that brings about manifestation.

In the case of addiction, we need to apply the law of relativity so that we remain positive all the time. Everyone who wants to get out of addiction believes that addiction is nothing but evil. However, this notion fills the person with negativity. We need to look at addiction from a different angle. Addiction indeed brings disaster to our lives, but it is also true that there was a time when addiction helped us overcome our insecurities and shortcomings. Addiction in itself is not solely a bad thing; it does have some positive aspects as well, but its negative aspects foreshadow the positive aspects, so it becomes compulsory to get rid of it.

The law of relativity can also be used to develop the thinking that you are blessed and have taken the step to get out of the addiction. Instead of looking at your past and thinking negatively about the addiction, you need to embrace the fact that numerous addicts haven't yet developed the courage to even think about taking a step away from addiction. You are lucky and blessed in this regard, so you must stay positive, attracting positive energy from the whole Universe.

Law of Inspired Action

This law advises that you must contribute to the creation to make your ambitions and desires a reality. This implies that you must take coordinated and inspired action to create your desires, whether large or tiny. While the law of attraction is concerned with vibrationally aligning yourself with whatever you desire, the law of inspired action is concerned with bringing what you desire to fruition.

Ultimately it all comes down to taking tangible measures to welcome our desires into our lives. Slowing down, being silent, and making space for internal direction are all part of practicing this law. When we let go of the urge to plan and control how things will turn out and remain open to all possibilities, we open the door to new methods of accomplishing our objectives that we may not have considered otherwise.

Because the Law of Attraction is not a mystical formula that magically converts your goals into reality, taking inspired action is crucial for your manifestation success. The Law of Attraction is built on a goal-setting and goal-achieving process that is reinforced through subconscious mind retraining. And nothing will happen until you take action.

Without taking the needed action, you can't fight addiction. Belief, imagination, and thoughts are critical and vital for manifestation. However, inspired action is also crucial. Without devising a plan of action and working according to the plan, you won't be able to bring about manifestation.

Law of Compensation

The law of compensation is strongly related to the laws of attraction and correspondence. The primary message is that "you reap what you sow." The law declares that a person will always be paid for his efforts and contributions, no matter what the effort, no matter how much or how little it is.

Your reward may not arrive immediately, all at once, or in the manner you intended, but it will arrive. What we have in mind determines how we apply compensation law. The consequences of compensating are amplified by strong belief and mental clarity.

The biggest hurdle we face while working toward our goal is getting discouraged when we don't see our efforts bearing any fruit. The law of compensation helps us with these feelings. Addiction is very challenging, so it is normal to feel discouraged while fighting it, even if you have a powerful mind. When we lose courage in such circumstances, the law of compensation comes to mind. We reassure ourselves that we might not be getting our reward immediately. Still, our efforts are indeed helping us move towards our goal. Soon enough, we will experience what we always had imagined.

Summary

The Universe loves law and order, so it has many laws working in close relation with each other to maintain the integrity of our Universe. Understanding these laws will allow us to benefit.

The first and foremost law of the Universe is that the mind holds the ultimate power. There is nothing more powerful than a mind in this Universe. When our mind becomes coherent with the Universe's energy, it attains the power to manifest what we imagine. However, to attain this power, we must harmonize our vibration with the Universe's vibration. Then, we will truly become part of the unending energy flow of the Universe which brings every part of this Universe to existence.

Another law of the Universe states that our external behavior is all the mirror image of what we have inside us. So to bring harmony to our life energy, we need to change ourselves from the inside. Every cause has an effect, and every effect becomes the cause of something else. There are no accidents in this world, and the results we make in our life are a direct outcome of causes that originate inside us. Without bringing about inner change, our external identity won't be any different.

We first need to accept change as a whole to bring change to ourselves. We need to accept all aspects of masculinity as well as femininity. We all have these characteristics; without accepting them, we can't become worthy enough to bring internal change.

However, this is where the theory of relativity will come to our assistance, which implies that we need to see our situation from a positive point of view. We might view the time taken to accept our true selves as a hostile gesture; however, this allows us to get to know ourselves more accurately, which will help in the acceptance.

When we attain our ultimate power of the mind, the law of attraction comes into play, which attracts positive energies to ourselves, amplifying our power which ultimately becomes so strong that we can imagine and bring that imagination into existence.

All the laws of the Universe are always present to help you in your journey toward a better and prosperous life; we need to learn about these laws and implement them in ourselves.

The Quantum Side

From the start of this book, I am talking about the quantum side of different concepts and laws of the universe. The concepts of quantum physics are very confusing and difficult to understand, so in this chapter, I will try to describe what I mean when I use the word "Quantum Side."

The term quantum refers to tiny particles that constitute everything in this world. The quantum aspect of things is what happens in your mind before it manifests physically. It is the starting point for everything. The quantum side focuses on getting our minds caught up in the Vortex, getting our minds on the same page as our positive desires, putting our past behind us, and concentrating on our future. The key to your quantum side of life and its destiny is to start living in the Vortex.

What is Vortex?

We have previously discussed that everything in this world has vibrational energy, and we can achieve anything by aligning our frequency with our desires. We all have a source from which we are born; you can call this source nature, the universe, the divine, or perhaps God. So, in compliance with the vibrational law, we can also align ourselves with the vibration of our source. Abraham Hicks terms our alignment with our source as the Vortex. When we align with our source, all the energy starts flowing into our bodies. So, a vortex can be called a stream of energy that originates from our source. It is an area, a place, or a dimension where all the vibrational energies, including the source energies, are aligned with one another. It's like an enclosed, compacted source of pure positive energy.

According to the universal law of fellowship, whenever two or more individuals with similar vibrations come together for the same goal, their cumulative energy gets amplified, becoming double, tripled, or even more than that. All the energies present in each of us have one core source, and that source is present in the Vortex. So, this is that unified place where your energy will get combined with the energies of others with a similar purpose, boosting it exponentially. Hence, getting into the Vortex means aligning yourself with your higher self or connecting yourself with the vibration of the Unified Field. A unified field is a realm with nothing but harmony with the power of creation itself.

The Vortex is the container for our dreams, aspirations, and goals until we achieve vibrational harmony with them. It's the everlasting reservoir of happiness to which every one of us has contributed significantly during our physical lives. The Vortex is as real as our dreams and goals; we can't see it; we can only feel it.

Living in the Vortex

Living in the Vortex implies a state of alignment that promotes magic and miracles. It's where you'll find creative solutions to your questions. It's the place where everything comes together flawlessly. It's the place where you feel on top of the world. Living in the Vortex has the benefit of making creativity, intuition, and manifestation automatic and effortless. When you are in harmony with the vibration of the source of creation, you have the power to manifest anything you desire effortlessly.

How you feel will tell you whether you're in or out of the Vortex. You're in when you feel wonderful. You're outside of it if you're feeling lousy. It would be best if you also took action from the Vortex. That "aligned" condition is a perfect moment to start working toward your objective. Because whatever you do outside of the Vortex is unlikely to provide the desired results. So getting in is critical if you want to live a life of comfort and flow, as purposeful creators do.

Getting into the Vortex

We have several bodies, and our spirit resides in multiple realms. To advance to the higher self, it is important to concentrate only on the mental, emotional, physical, and spiritual bodies. The path you take to enter the Vortex may vary from that of others. There are, however, many techniques through which you can enter the Vortex. You can try meditation, one of the most effective ways to gain entry into the Vortex. Moreover, being kind, positive affirmations, visualization, and practicing yoga can also be beneficial.

All these techniques will always have one thing in common: whenever you do any of these things, you will feel good about yourself and bring your mental, emotional and spiritual bodies together. So, the simplest way to enter the Vortex is to do things that make you feel good about yourself.

For example, whenever I feel low, I go to the gym. I spend multiple hours there, working out and pushing my body to the limits. I lift weights, walk on the treadmill, jog a little, go back to exercising, look in the mirror, and flex. Doing all these exercises and watching myself flex in the mirror makes me feel good. It makes me lively. Being in the gym allows me to release all the pressure and stress. It allows me to flush out all the negativity and misleading energies. This brings vibrational harmony to my mind, body, and spirit, allowing me to enter the quantum side and the Vortex.

Resistance

Vortex works on the principle of the Law of Attraction. It attracts you; it tries to engulf you all by itself. It's you who hinders its attraction. You pose resistance at the entrance of this realm. So how do you cause hindrance? By holding onto your old ways of living, by working too hard.

Let's take the example of cork. Cork is porous and made of wood and floats easily on the water. Even the ripples generated in its vicinity are unable to submerge it. Now, you put resistance or pressure on the cork with your hand. This pressure makes it submerge under water. The main purpose of the cork was to float, and it was already there, but the resistance provided by your hand has caused it to deviate from its main purpose.

Similarly, you are already near a vortex and attracted to it, but two things pose resistance in your way. One is your old ways of living. When you don't let go of yourself, you won't be able to align with your higher self. The resistance you pose comes when you refuse to accept change or let go of the past.

The second resistance is confusion, the process of overdoing it. When you have left your old ways and have accepted the change, as stated above, you have reached your destination. You are already on the verge of entering the Vortex. Your hope and belief in yourself have made you eligible for entry into the Vortex. But when you start procrastinating, become confused, and doubt your eligibility, you create resistance. The door to the Vortex is somewhere between hope and belief. You have the hope to enter the Vortex, but when you doubt yourself, you stop believing in yourself, and this causes problems. So remember, you are already in the quantum realm; you are already in the Vortex; you need to let go of your old ways and believe in yourself. Just align yourself with the universe's vibrations, and you will have all the power at your disposal.

Quantum Side is a new way of life. Where we no longer identify ourselves or make decisions based on horror stories of the past. The quantum side is establishing a mindset of love and abundance and restructuring our lives. Words, actions, smells, and feelings trigger past Patterns. These rehearsed horror stories are to be written in books and left there for anyone curious to read and learn from them. On the quantum side, we abandon old irrelevant ways of living as we learn to apply the laws that govern us on a clean, fresh slate.

Letting go of the past

Nobody can deny that there has been a moment or episode in their life when they wished situations had been different. We all have regrets; we all have incidents and decisions in our past lives that we want to change. However, moving back to your past is not an option on the journey toward a better life. What you need to understand is that the past is done. You don't have the power to travel back in time and change what you did. But you have all the power to alter your present and future. So focus on your present, let go of the past, and let go of your horror stories. Please don't get stuck on it.

Although the past is essential because we learn from it and build the present and future, it should not be too intrusive in our goals, or it will become a hindrance rather than a help. We must let go of things that have gone before to live in the present. Everything has a time and a place, and the events that have transpired in the past were predestined. Seeking them in the present for all the wrong reasons stifles development.

Getting stuck in the past is easy because it gives you the easy way out. It allows you to play the victim card. It allows you to curse your fortune and the world for what has happened to you.

By staying in the past, you put all the blame on others. For example, you blame the universe for putting you in a bad neighborhood; you blame the universe for giving you a rough life when someone else is living in luxury. You blame the universe for providing you with a negative environment that played a part in your misery.

It doesn't matter how easy and convenient staying in the past might seem. It is not an option. Going back to your past will initiate the domino effect. As soon as you open the door to your past, you start losing everything you have. You start losing your family, friends, car, house, and the list goes on. The dominoes will keep on falling, one forcing the other to fall.

Letting go of the past is not an easy feat to accomplish, and the reason for this is that the past is always calling you. There is always a way for the past to entice you back to it. It will keep welcoming you, saying, "We miss you; where have you been?" It will keep on putting force on the cord to pull you back. But remember that you have the power to let it go. You are the one who created your past; you are the creator. Although the past wants you back, you can win over your horror stories with determination and focus.

The Power of New Beginning

We see life as a straight line with a definite beginning, middle, and finish. We are born, spend our lives as we see fit, and then die. However, with a simple shift of perspective, that line can be transformed into a sequence of circles, making our life cyclical, beginning, middle, end, and repeat.

Every end is a new beginning, and we are given a fresh perspective. Putting an end to our past will bring about the beginning. Beginnings have a tremendous inherent power that can be harnessed if used appropriately. Have you ever noticed that most diets begin on Monday more than any other day? You feel a rush of energy in your body when you think of the beginning of a new week. What makes you believe that? Because new beginnings provide individuals with strength, perspective, and a fresh start.

New Year's Day is the epitome of a beginning. The page has turned, your canvas is clean, the year has ended, and a new one has begun. Just thinking about the New Year explodes our minds with numerous thoughts about how we want to spend this New Year and what we want to achieve in it. This is the power of beginning. It gives you the energy to transform your present.

Beginning constructs a bridge between your present and what you desire to achieve. Once this bridge has been constructed, all you have to do is keep making efforts and moving forward toward the life of abundance you have always wanted. One thing to remember is that going backward is not an option; you only need to move forward.

This beginning is what the quantum side is all about. It is all about transforming your present into what you desire. As soon as you have decided to put a stop to your past and bring about the beginning of eliminating your bad habit, you have entered the quantum realm. Where we no longer identify with or make decisions based on horror stories of the past.

Just as we walk away from bad memories, we begin to walk into new memories that haven't yet occurred. How is this possible? The brain does not know the difference between a thought/dream or an actual physical event. It's all about a feeling we receive from this thought that makes it relevant. Creativity is an expression of clear intent and an elevated feeling.

The key to the quantum side of life is to have a goal. Instead of drifting around to and fro, a goal, dream, or quest gives us purpose, reason, and direction. Direction is essential in life because without direction; there is nowhere to go, nothing to achieve, and no purpose.

Importance of Goal Setting

Many people feel disoriented in the world. They work hard, yet they never seem to achieve anything meaningful. They have a vague desire to alter bad habits, but they don't seem to be making any progress. One of the main reasons people feel this way is that they haven't spent enough time thinking about what they want out of life and haven't created specific objectives for themselves. After all, would you go on an important journey if you had no clue where you were going?

Goal setting is a powerful method for seeing your ideal Goal setting is a powerful method for seeing your ideal future and inspiring yourself to make that vision a reality. Setting objectives allows you to decide where you want to go in life. You can focus your efforts more effectively by knowing precisely what you want to accomplish. You'll also see the diversions that might easily lead you astray.

The neurons in your brain form a complex pathway known as the "Reticular Activating System." Its function is to get stimulus from your environment and bring it to your attention. So, it plays a vital role in setting and achieving your goals. Fortunately, you can train your RAS by setting an intention. In other words, you can train by forming a link between your conscious and subconscious. This implies that if you concentrate hard on your objectives, your RAS will expose the information, people, and chances that will assist you in achieving them. This training is similar to any physical training. The more and more you train your reticular activating system, the easier it will become for your brain to detect and expose the relevant people and information.

Having a clear, compelling purpose directs your attention to actionable behavior. Goal setting, in other words, motivates you. For example, you have a keen desire to eliminate your bad habits, but whenever someone asks you when you want your bad habits to be gone, your most probable reply will be "as soon as possible." In this case, you have a strong desire to achieve something but lack a defined goal. The issue here is that the result isn't clear. Conversely, if you are more specific, I will start using the power of my mind and imagination and eliminate these bad habits before next year starts. Now you have something to aspire to; you have a mental cue that triggers your focus and motivates you to use the power of the mind.

The most beneficial aspect of goal setting is its ability to improve your focus. Without a purpose, your efforts will be scattered and often misleading. A goal, for example, takes a hummingbird's wild and erratic flight and focuses it, much like a hawk that swoops down for its prey. This means that your actions will be chaotic and irregular at the start after setting the goal. You will face some difficulty in finding a way to achieve your goal. But as soon as you figure out the way, your focus will be amplified, and you will start moving towards your destination with motivation and courage, ultimately achieving your goal.

So, why is the aspect of the focus the most beneficial? Because the focus is the key to manifestation.

Importance of focus

As I have discussed earlier, the mind is the most powerful part of our body, and it has the power to bring about manifestation. However, certain factors amplify its power. One such important factor is the focus. Having something to focus on is essential for the proper growth of the mind. Focus is important because it is the gateway to all thinking, perception, memory learning, reasoning, problem-solving, and decision-making. Without good focus, all aspects of your ability to think will suffer. Focus guides the mind through its capability of filtering important information and moving it up the ladder for deeper processing while suppressing interruptions through a function known as efficient selection. So basically, everything is a distraction if you don't have anything to focus on. These distractions cause an imbalance in the optimum working of the mind and act as obstacles toward manifestation

What happens is that when you don't have a focus, your brain dissects everything and gives you emotional feelings about certain things that are irrelevant. This happens because your brain has nothing to grab onto. The brain becomes curious. The brain says you know what, let's find things. Instead of building synapses around your main focus, the brain forms synapses around stuff that doesn't matter. Thus, dissecting and dividing the power of the mind to work on multiple things simultaneously leads to no gain.

For example, let's assume you get a project to build a five-star restaurant. Now, if you develop a keen focus on this project, you will dedicate your mind solely to the restaurant. Throughout the project, you will analyze your methods and work to find new ways to improve your approach to make this restaurant the best it can be. Your robust focus on this project will ensure you don't get distracted by the problems and drama in your surroundings. You will concentrate all the power of your mind on manifesting your imagination and achieving the best result.

The key to life is to think our way into our true desires, think our way out of bad habits, and think our way into a new reality of love and abundance. There's nothing an idea can't solve. An idea is a breakthrough resolution. Ideas come from imagination, and imagination is formed from the level of vibrations we connect with, establishing the frequencies that determine our manifestation.

Theta State

The power of imagination comes in a state called **Theta**. Our brain has five waves: Beta, Alpha, Theta, Delta, and Gamma. Theta is a state of mind that is associated with the power of imagination and the power of manifestation. This state is a kind of state of hypnosis.

If you have driven a vehicle over long distances, you can easily understand this concept of theta state. While driving, you might encounter a phase in which you are thinking about something deeply or becoming drowsy. When you get out of this phase, you don't remember anything that happened in the previous 5-10 minutes.

What happens is that when you are in this state of relaxation, your mind frequency gets very low, and you enter into a state of sleep, except that a small part of your brain is still conscious. An important thing to notice here is that, in this state of mind, you don't encounter any accidents; although you are not completely conscious, your body is working on its own.

In the theta state, the brain produces theta waves. The subconscious is governed by theta brain waves, which regulate the portion of our mind that falls between the conscious and the unconscious and preserves memories and emotions. These waves direct your thoughts and conduct as well. Theta waves are filled with feelings of creativity and are highly spiritual. This mental state enables you to behave below the level of your conscious mind.

Harnessing theta waves can help you visualize your objectives and bring them to reality. Theta frequency increases when you consciously exercise creativity, self-regulation, and brain-building, notably at frontal locations during tasks that demand attention or short-term memory. It's vital to remember that theta waves are an energy reaction to mental activity, and how we control our brains determines how well we respond to theta waves. This is where our actual authenticity lives, where we can reconnect with the universe and discover the essence of who we are, what we desire, and what we need to be. Manifesting becomes easy once we reach this stage. So, Theta is a state of perfect calm and serenity, in which your mind is completely free and whatever you imagine or think in this state manifests itself into reality.

How to Enter Theta State

There are two ways you can reach the Theta state. One is that if you set some form of sound or alarm that activates your mundane thinking while sleeping, you may wake yourself up from the deep Delta sleep state and start a dream state, and you get the capacity to enter dreams at choice or if you're dreaming at night, you can reach Theta.

When you are awake and want to shut down that rational hyperactive mind and enter that epiphany state and that highly creative state, you may attain Theta by sitting in a calm condition.

Assume you've been working all day and now want to relax. Sit in a comfortable position. Maintain complete silence while holding a ball in your hand. Begin to forget about your work and worries. Relax in your position, which indicates you're moving from Gamma to Beta to Alpha. You calm your mind, and then you allow yourself to get drowsy. You would begin to let your mind enter this type of fantasy, enumeration mode. But keep in mind that you don't want to fall asleep. You don't want to nod off and become unconscious. So, as soon as you begin to go into that Delta, that deep state, your hand would relax, and the ball would be knocked down, waking you up from that Delta to that Theta state. You will experience a lot of epiphanies at these times, which you may utilize to practice imagination, visualization, and tapping into the power of manifestation.

Summary

There are two ways you can reach the Theta state. One is that if you set some form of sound or alarm that activates your mundane thinking while sleeping, you may wake yourself up from the deep Delta sleep state and start a dream state, and you get the capacity to enter dreams at choice or if you're dreaming at night, you can reach Theta.

When you are awake and want to shut down that rational hyperactive mind and enter that epiphany state and that highly creative state, you may attain Theta by sitting in a calm condition.

Assume you've been working all day and now want to relax. Sit in a comfortable position. Maintain complete silence while holding a ball in your hand. Begin to forget about your work and worries. Relax in your position, which indicates you're moving from Gamma to Beta to Alpha. You calm your mind, and then you allow yourself to get drowsy. You would begin to let your mind enter this type of fantasy, enumeration mode. But keep in mind that you don't want to fall asleep. You don't want to nod off and become unconscious. So, as soon as you begin to go into that Delta, that deep state, your hand would relax, and the ball would be knocked down, waking you up from that Delta to that Theta state. You will experience a lot of epiphanies at these times, which you may utilize to practice imagination, visualization, and tapping into the power of manifestation. Our cosmos loves absolute, ubiquitous, consistent, and neutral laws and principles. We may claim ignorance of the complicated workings of these rules. But, whether we are conscious of it or not, we are constantly engaging with and using these principles in our lives.

Subconsciously, we all know these divine laws of the universe. These principles and laws are the backbones of the universe's working body. This chapter will teach us about the universe's laws to understand its complexity.

Laws of the universe are essential because they bring nature into balance and harmony. You will better understand how the universe operates if you learn these laws. Once you've learned the rules, you can apply them to your personal life to advance prosperity. Every universal rule is a piece of the complicated jigsaw that is the universe. They are all linked and operate together. As such, they can guide making the most of life. Let's take a closer look at the universal laws, how they affect our life, and how you may use them to your advantage.

Creating a Wining Environment

What forces some atoms to transform into precious shining crystals and gemstones while most atoms only make dull rocks? One answer. The right environment. You might wonder why I am suddenly talking about crystals out of nowhere. Well, let's dive deeper. Crystals are made up of highly organized atoms or molecules under immense temperature and pressure.

Atoms need a specific environment to transform into an incredible and visually appealing matter. The physical qualities of the crystal make it stand out among other stones. An atom can make either transit into a fascinating crystal or remain an ordinary stone, depending on its environment. I am sure now you're getting where I am going.

We, like crystals, need a winning environment. Why? Because the right environment can help you discover your deepest talents.

A winning environment implies a positivity-filled environment that helps you succeed in all aspects of your life. In our war against our bad habits, we must utilize all of our weapons to win. A winning environment is one of those weapons. The science behind this concept is that the environmental cues or the objects in our surroundings trigger certain thoughts and desires, causing us to behave in certain ways, to do something out of the ordinary. We can't recover in the same environment where we formed our bad habits as that environment cues us to revert to those habits. We need to create a winning environment that prompts us to keep working towards success.

The environment always affects you, whether positively or negatively. If you pack your bags right now and go to live in a place where everyone around you is rich, it wouldn't take long before you would pick up some of their traits. So, if we surround ourselves with positivity, we foster positivity in all aspects of our life.

Our brain works in a way where it says you know what? This is a comfort zone, and we become wired to stay in the same place. When we create a winning environment, we try new things. During this process, our brain destroys wiring from the damaging environment, enabling us to become wired to this new, positive, and successful environment.

Science has discovered something awesome. No longer are we imprisoned by our genes or family sickness or health. But, by the environment we place ourselves in. This phenomenon is called **Epigenetics.**

Epigenetics tells us that everything happening to us on our genetic level is because of our environment. We are not victims of bad habits because our parents were. We are here only because we choose to be, only because we think it's inevitable. To grow and eliminate our bad habits, we must destroy this mindset. Epigenetics is the science that tells us how the environment can become our biggest savior.

Every cell of our body, except the red blood cells, contains a nucleus with chromatids. Chromatids are compressed and entangled forms of our DNA or genes. Now epigenetics states that an environment filled with abuse of drugs triggers an alteration or mutation in our genes which causes us to develop an addiction. You didn't have a craving for drugs when you hadn't started using them, so then why do you get them now? Because your environment has mutated your genes. This all might seem overwhelming to you, but there is a silver lining for you in epigenetics. The opposite can also be true if an environment filled with bad habits can change our genes and develop cravings. We can eliminate cravings and bad habits by changing our environment and reversing the mutations. So, this chapter is about how you can create a winning environment that will reverse your mutations and bring success.

How to Create a Winning Environment?

Before we learn how to create a winning environment, we should learn what an environment is. When you hear the word environment, the concept that will pop into your mind is that it is everything that is around us physically. You think the house, the people, and the air around us are the environments. Well, you are partially right.

Our environment is not limited to the surroundings of our bodies. Our environment includes our body, our mind, and our spirit, along with our surroundings. So, in this chapter, I will discuss how to create a winning environment concerning your body, mind, and spirit. Dealing with all three aspects of yourself is important. Your body, mind, and spirit make you the whole. Healing one while ignoring the other won't offer optimal health.

Part 01: The Body

When recovering, we fill ourselves with foods to regain weight. When we detox from drugs, our bodies are like a sponge. They absorb things quickly, and they put them to use quickly. So a lot of times, what we do is fill ourselves up with all types of unhealthy foods just because we're hungry.

Over time, our bad habits can leave us with a weak immune system. When our defense falls, we get more prone to infections, diseases, and disorders. Drug abuse can lead to numerous heart conditions, including arrhythmia, collapsed arteries and veins, heart attack, and an increased risk of infection of the cardiac muscles. Other severely impacted organs include the liver, kidney, lungs, and gastrointestinal tract.

Your appearance is a mirror of your internal world. When organs struggle to do their job, it shows in a person's complexion, hair, nails, teeth, and weight. Acne, skin lesions, baldness, or male pattern hair growth in women are frequent side effects. Problems with the jaw and teeth, such as cavities and gum disease, have also been reported by many individuals. These alterations can cause difficulties in daily life, and it's critical to healing all of our body's damaged building blocks.

They delight our tongues, taste lovely at the moment, and are also quite effective at suppressing uncomfortable feelings. But, as we all know, junk foods make us unwell. They deplete our energy, cause us to gain weight, and make us feel displaced.

The same is true for the mind. We often have many thoughts that are like junk food. These are the negative thoughts. For example, judging and criticizing someone feels good at the moment, but it damages us. It feeds our smallness and restricts us from facing our fears and developing courage.

The food we eat affects all of our bodies, including our minds. When we eat something, it gets absorbed into the blood, crosses the blood-brain barrier, and reaches the brain. The brain gets the same effect that the food poses inside it. If we eat healthy food, our brains will stay healthy, giving rise to healthy thoughts. But, if we fill our stomachs with unhealthy junk food, the same unhealthy thoughts will pop up in our minds.

We can treat all these conditions individually or find an easy way to correct them simultaneously. A proper diet is the best way to return our body to a healthy state and benefit our mind from a work regime that is performed by a healthy body. So, here I have put together some foods and vitamins that can heal your body quickly.

Foods to abolish

As our body acts like a sponge after the detox, consuming unhealthy foods can worsen our conditions, whereas healthy foods can heal our bodies quickly. It is the perfect opportunity to get extra healthy. First, I will talk about the foods you should restrain yourself from.

Sugar

I advise you to stay miles away from sugar if you can. Sugar is the best drug on the market right now. People in recovery frequently crave it because it gives short comfort from low blood sugar. But, consuming sugar exacerbates the health problem since it has no nutritional value and deprives the body of essential minerals and vitamins—no wonder sugar is famously known as the white poison among nutritionists.

Sugar clogs your brain, causes erectile dysfunction for guys, and causes a whole array of things to your body. High blood sugar levels can lead to insulin resistance, resulting in type 2 diabetes. Moreover, sugar is nothing more than empty calories. We crowd out nutrients by consuming ultra-processed high sugar and carb food like ice cream, fried food, cakes, sweets, etc. It depletes our bodies of crucial nutrients necessary for a healthy immune system and metabolism. The presence of sugar also depletes chromium, zinc, magnesium, and copper from the body.

Blood sugar and mood are inextricably linked, particularly blood sugar spikes and lows—the more irregular your blood glucose, the more erratic your mood. You won't get the key amino acids and vitamins you need to help your mood if you eat a high-sugar, low-nutrient diet. Sugar intake can thus lead to depression.

Sugar in the blood destroys the elastin and collagen strands that keep your skin supple. This fact in itself should deter you from ever eating sugar again!

It may be the case that artificial sweeteners come into your mind when I discuss cutting off sugar. Although artificial sweeteners can help diabetes patients, they are detrimental to your health. Try to replace sugar with natural sweeteners. The best sugar alternative is raw honey, which has many health benefits. You can also use molasses, pure maple syrup, or even the coconut sugar I use.

Caffeine

Caffeine has been proven guilty in studies of causing addiction. Caffeine's addictive characteristics are influenced by the quantity you drink daily and the potency of what you drink. For example, a cup of coffee has around 100mg of caffeine, whereas energy drinks have approximately 75 to 90mg.

When inherent predispositions to addictive behaviors are combined, developing a caffeine addiction is a serious risk for someone who regularly consumes excessive quantities of caffeine. Caffeine has recognized addictive components, and many individuals in recovery utilize it for replacing their former drug usage. Therefore, avoiding excessive caffeine use while in recovery is critical.

Coffee impairs your body's capability to absorb certain vitamins. It has been proven to limit vitamin D, calcium, and potassium absorption, all of which are necessary for your recovery.

Caffeine can trigger your brain to overproduce stress-inducing chemicals. These include adrenaline and acetylcholine, which can cause anxiety and stress when in excess.

Drinking three to four cups of coffee daily can severely damage your kidneys and liver. Also, it is very bad for patients with high blood pressure and creates excess mucus. However, coffee is an excellent stimulant to wake up your brain early in the morning. So, if you can't completely abolish its use, try to reduce its consumption until you get rid of it. That's precisely what I did.

I have completely gotten rid of coffee. I replaced it entirely with a healthy alternative, mushroom coffee, because it is good for our brain and immune system and its stimulant properties. Caffeine avoidance guarantees that your mind and body can mend correctly throughout recovery without relying on another drug.

White Flour

Here's another white poison in your kitchen cabinet that you must avoid. White flour acts like processed sugar. It is made by removing the most nutrient-rich parts of the flour, which are the bran and the germ, so the only things left are mainly carbohydrates. It lacks fiber, clogs the system, delays digestion, resulting in a sluggish metabolism, and impairs the body's regular functioning. Its consumption can result in metabolic syndrome, constipation, increased stress levels, and migraine. It is very easy to replace white flour in your diet. You can use whole grain flour, brown rice flour, rye flour, or spelt flour as a healthy alternative.

Fats

Although fats usually have a bad reputation, not all fats are bad for health. The harmful fats are hydrogenated and refined fats, also known as trans-fats. Fats are hydrogenated to increase their stability and thus improve their shelf life. It is also preferred for its low cost, so numerous processed foods have hydrogenated fat as a common ingredient. Studies reveal that hydrogenated fats increase bad cholesterol (Low-density lipoproteins) and decrease good cholesterol (High-density Lipoprotein), adversely affecting one's heart.

Meat

Although meat is considered a good source of protein, it contains insanely high levels of bad fats. Moreover, meat contains certain hormones. These hormones of the animals are mainly similar to the hormones produced in our bodies. So, meat consumption can cause an imbalance of hormones, altering our body's normal functioning and cycle. Once we connect and are aligned with what's natural for us, we can fully evolve. I've been a vegetarian for over a year and noticed that my craving for unhealthy substances, including sugar, has been drastically erased.

Often, we consume food without questioning its ingredients. Just because your food looks aesthetic does not mean it would be good for your body. You can't attain full recovery without eliminating all the factors that cause damage. Your food choices might be the biggest obstacle on your road to recovery.

Vitamins and Minerals

Vitamins and minerals are essential nutrients for the optimum functioning of the body. They are involved in body metabolism, normal cell functioning, digestion, disease prevention, and regulating the body's internal environment. These nutrients are required in small amounts, so we can get them from the food and beverages we consume daily. However, not every food has all the vitamins and minerals. So, you can develop a deficiency of certain minerals in your body if you consume the same and limited foods for many years.

Certain illicit substances can hinder the absorption of vital minerals and vitamins, even if your food contains them. For example, excessive consumption of alcohol damages the internal lining of the intestines, which absorbs almost all the nutrients you get from foods into your bloodstream. This damage interferes with the absorption capability of the intestine, causing the expulsion of vital nutrients from the body without getting absorbed in adequate amounts. So, prolonged use of alcohol causes deficiency which is critical to counter for optimum recovery.

Moreover, people with bad habits often lose their appetite for normal food. They consume less food without paying attention to their diet's constituents. Usually, they crave unhealthy junk food. So, their diet doesn't have an adequate amount of vital nutrients, leading to vitamin and mineral deficiencies. Even though multivitamin pills can provide beneficial vitamins and minerals; some require more attention than others. Here is a list of key minerals and vitamins that must be considered in recovery.

Water-soluble Vitamins

As the name suggests, these vitamins are soluble in water. And so they can be easily excreted from the body by the kidneys. Their water solubility gives them the advantage of not being toxic, meaning that if taken in excess amounts, these vitamins are easily excreted from the body through urine. However, their water-soluble property doesn't allow them to be stored in large amounts; therefore, these vitamins must be taken regularly.

B Vitamins

There are eight B vitamins, ranging from B1 to B12. All these vitamins are necessary and play a key role in producing neurotransmitters and the brain's normal functioning. Although vitamin B deficiency can occur because of irregular food consumption, alcohol consumption can also be an important factor. Alcohol causes the breakdown of vitamin B, especially thiamine (B1), and a prolonged thiamine deficiency can lead to nerve damage.

Taking vitamin B-containing food and supplements can have many beneficial effects for people undergoing recovery. Research has revealed that Vitamin B supplementation can positively affect cognitive function because it lowers the Hcy levels. Homocysteine (Hcy) is an amino acid whose elevation damages the brain.

Its supplementation will have beneficial effects on the other parts of the body as well. These include better digestion and absorption of other nutrients, an increase in the body's power level and decrease in lethargy, lower stress levels, improved metabolism, and detoxification.

So, what do you need to eat to maintain the level of B vitamins in your body? Almost all the multivitamin preparations on the market contain multiple B vitamins. Still, it is important to check whether all eight vitamins B are present in the product. You can also buy B complex supplements containing only vitamin B. Foods like leafy vegetables, legumes, whole grains, and bananas are good sources of B vitamins.

Vitamin C

This is the gold vitamin while recovering from bad habits. Vitamin C aids in detoxification while decreasing drug cravings. It also strengthens your immune system, which drug abuse has weakened. Oxidative damage in the body has a detrimental effect on the brain and compromises the mind's capability. Therefore, as an antioxidant, vitamin C is also helpful for the brain.

Vitamin C is stored in various tissues throughout the body, with the adrenal glands having the largest quantities. The adrenal glands, which sit above the kidneys, secrete vitamin C and cortisol, the hormone that gives us the emotional fortitude we need to deal with stress. However, this response has a negative side as well. As the stress increases, more stored vitamin C gets secreted into the blood, leading to its deficiency. Using illicit substances dramatically contributes to stress, so their use can deplete stored Vitamin C.

Vitamin C, also known as Ascorbic acid, is present in sour food, like citrus fruits. It is also present in strawberries, currants, cruciferous vegetables, and tomatoes. Supplements of Vitamin C are also readily available. The recommended daily limit of vitamin C is 2000 mg. I take two tablets of 1000mg of Vitamin C supplements daily in the morning. Increased intake doesn't cause any issues because it just comes out when you go to the bathroom.

Fat-soluble Vitamins

These vitamins are soluble in fat and can remain stored in the body in large amounts. Moreover, consuming an excess amount of these vitamins can be toxic, so these vitamins must be taken in limited amounts.

Vitamin D

This vitamin performs several functions in the body, including bone growth, calcium absorption, immune system boost, and muscle function. Vitamin D is the only vitamin that our bodies can produce when exposed to sunshine. Therefore, people living in the northern hemisphere, where less ultraviolet light reaches the ground during the winter, make less vitamin D. This increases the risk of vitamin D deficiency.

It is a common misconception that people with darker skin tones make more vitamin D. This is certainly not the case. Melanin is the substance that gives skin color, and darker-skinned people have more of it than lighter-skinned people. More melanin lowers your capacity to manufacture vitamin D from sunlight. So, Vitamin D supplementation for people with a darker skin tone, like me, is very important, especially in the recovery process.

Vitamin D supplementation tablets are also very readily available. The sources of vitamin D also include egg yolks, yoghurt, and cheese.

Vitamin E

Due to its anti-oxidative property, vitamin E decreases significantly in the body due to drug usage. Drugs like heroin, cocaine, and alcohol contain many harmful oxidative compounds. When these compounds enter the body, Vitamin E starts warding them off. In this battle, the bad guys are likely to overpower vitamin E when they are huge in numbers.

This antioxidant determines our immune health and cellular signaling in our body. Daily vitamin E intake lower than 1000 mg doesn't have any damaging effects; however, surpassing this threshold can cause dizziness, nausea, fatigue, and bleeding. Some vitamin E sources, besides supplementation pills, are sunflower seeds and oil, almonds, peanuts, pumpkin, avocados, spinach, and red bell pepper.

Mineral

Iron

Iron present in the red blood cells helps them to carry oxygen from the lungs to all the parts of the body. It is also crucial in the production of new blood cells. Iron keeps you warm in winter and glowing in the summer.

Drugs destroy red blood cells in your body. So, people with bad habits are often anemic. Therefore, iron supplementation is vital for improving the production of red blood cells and treating anemia. Almonds, broccoli, spinach, cereals, beans, and peanuts are excellent sources of iron. Large amounts of iron can be toxic, so limit yourself to consuming less than 40-45 mg daily.

Calcium and Magnesium

Calcium and magnesium are two minerals that are closely related and may be adversely affected by drug or alcohol addiction. Calcium and magnesium are essential in the formation and breakdown of bone mass, as well as in muscular contraction and relaxation. Magnesium is a mineral that is utilized in the metabolism of alcohol, which causes magnesium loss. These lower-than-normal readings might appear as withdrawal symptoms such as tremors, muscular cramps, and changes in heart rhythm.

Calcium-rich foods include legumes, dairy products, and leafy green vegetables. Whole grains, leafy green vegetables, seaweed, okra, tamarind, nuts, and seeds all contain magnesium. Large amounts of calcium can be toxic to the heart, so limit yourself to 1000-1200 mg daily. Similarly, take up to 350-420 mg of the daily dose of magnesium in your diet.

Zinc

Zinc, like magnesium, is substantially utilized in the metabolization of alcohol. Zinc deficiency can impair eyesight, wound healing, and appetite leading to depression. Legumes, eggs, nuts, and whole grains are all excellent sources of zinc. The daily dose of zinc is between 8-11 mg.

Other supplements

Fish oil

Fish oil contains omega-3 and omega-6 fatty acids, which activate the body's natural healing process. When we take addictive drugs, our brain cells are directly affected. Fish oil helps in the healing and regeneration of brain cells. It is readily available in the market in transparent pills or capsules. I take two of these pills daily.

Lion's Mane Mushroom

Lion's mane mushrooms contain compounds that stimulate the growth of brain cells and protect them from damage caused by substance dependency. It helps support brain health, boosts the immune system, and promotes natural energy levels. It is a powerful neurotropic; in simpler terms, you can take it to relieve symptoms of stress and depression. It is not toxic at high doses, but it is wise to take 750 mg daily.

Foods to include in the diet for recovery

So, now that we have discussed the foods we must avoid and the supplements that will help our recovery. It is time to discuss specific foods you must incorporate into your daily diet to achieve a healthy body and mind.

As I have discussed earlier, our body is like a sponge with increased absorption power when we fight our habits. We are now at a great advantage because we can make beneficial decisions. Now, we have fresh and fertile ground to build upon. The steps that we take from now on will alter our lives for the better. Through its spongy nature, our body has allowed us to make it healthy and grow easier than ever before. So, start eating healthy and witness the transformation of your life.

The way your brain thinks is supported by your stomach. It would not be wrong to say the stomach is your second brain. If you've ever had a gut feeling, that's your stomach thinking. So, it would be best if you treated it like a child, giving it all the necessary nourishment. If you want to be really on point with your emotions and prevent depression and anxiety, you should take good care of your gut. What you eat is extremely important for your grey matter as well. So here are some meals that are incredibly beneficial for your gut and brain.

Avocados

Avocados are delicious, versatile, and full of nutrients. Doctors usually recommend it to individuals with nervous disorders because of its neuroprotective abilities. The most crucial constituents of avocado are monounsaturated and polyunsaturated fat. Studies have revealed that monounsaturated fats protect the glial cells of the brain, which have a supportive role in information-carrying nerves. Monounsaturated fats also improve the brain's ability to control muscles. These fats are also perfect for maintaining healthy blood flow, which benefits the brain. Moreover, avocados contain a good amount of fiber, lowering your bad cholesterol level.

Avocados are rich in vitamins B, C, E, and K, along with magnesium and potassium. Moreover, the presence of fats also helps improve the absorption of fat-soluble nutrients. Avocados have anti-oxidative properties, and studies have revealed that they are especially good for the eyes. Avocados are also an excellent source of folate. Low folate levels are linked with depression.

Adding avocados to your diet is very easy because their versatility allows them to be incorporated into many recipes.

Blueberries

Blueberries are also known as brain berries because of their promising effects on the brain. They protect your brain against oxidative stress. Blueberries also shield you from brain disorders like dementia and Alzheimer's. They are like the fountain of youth that makes your brain young and active.

Blueberries are great for you if you have been consuming too much sugar. They will fulfil your craving for sugar to some extent while also reversing the adverse effects. They have carbs that stay in the blood for a short time and reduce spiking glucose levels.

I use blueberries early in the morning. You must start your day with a healthy meal because your body regenerates itself while you sleep. The brain has a liquid from your spine that washes your brain while you sleep, so when you wake up in the morning, your brain is fresh. Instead of hitting it with fried bacon and home fries with a lot of grease, it is better to use a blueberry, ginger smoothie, and spinach.

Broccoli

My love for broccoli is especially because of its vitamin K reserves which enhance cognitive functions, and its remarkable low-calorie source of dietary fiber.

Bad habits usually cause an absence of mind and forgetfulness. So, broccoli has anti-amnesic properties, which enhance memory and aid in focusing. The sulforaphane in broccoli is also great for healing damaged brain cells.

Protein is vital for the body. A large portion of our body is made up of protein, and so we need protein when we want our body to recover. It is a common misconception that you can only get protein from animals. You can also get protein from plants; even animals get their protein from plants, so we consume plant protein indirectly. Broccoli, avocado, salmon, and eggs have a high quantity of protein.

Although broccoli can be eaten raw, retaining all the mentioned nutrients while cooking broccoli is very important. Cooking broccoli with just a splash of water and lightly sautéed with garlic results in healthy, crunchy, and delicious broccoli.

Eggs

Many people eat eggs for breakfast because they are a simple source of protein, but eggs are also an excellent food for brain health. Eggs are high in various nutrients associated with brain function, including vitamins B6 and B12, folate, and choline. Choline, a precursor of acetylcholine, is abundant in egg yolks. Acetylcholine is required for cognitive functions such as memory, focus, and concentration and for sustaining a positive mood. So eggs are your cheerleaders.

Choline can also function as a bile salt, aiding in the absorption of fat-soluble substances essential for brain function, such as vitamins E, K1, and K2.

Opt for pasture-raised organic eggs, which are high in omega-3 fatty acids. The most important omega-3 fatty acid in eggs is DHA because your grey matter (layer of the brain) is made of DHA. Furthermore, omega-3 fatty acids are anti-inflammatory and can reduce blood clotting risk, reducing strokes.

Egg yolks turn on healthy cholesterol required to produce vitamin D and many hormones. Eggs retain more constituents when they encounter low heat, so poached and boiled eggs are the healthiest. Although I still eat eggs, it is a part of my diet that I eventually want to eliminate because I have become vegetarian. There is no doubt that eggs are good for your health, but if you are not comfortable eating them, you can get rid of them.

Green Leafy vegetables

Leafy green vegetables include kale, spinach, collard greens, cabbage, arugula, romaine lettuce, etc. They are high in B vitamins such as B6, B12, and folate. B vitamins are required for proper nerve and brain function. Because of these vitamins, leafy greens are a diet that successfully combats memory loss. In addition to B vitamins, leafy greens are abundant in minerals. They have been associated with a lower risk of heart disease and high blood pressure.

L-glutamine is an amino acid that has immunological and antioxidant properties. L-glutamine can help minimize sugar cravings, which are frequent in the early stages of recovery. Leafy green vegetables are excellent for increasing L-glutamine levels.

Anxiety, restlessness, and sleeplessness are classic symptoms of early recovery that often accompany withdrawal. By increasing GABA levels, leafy green foods like raw spinach can help reduce and counterbalance these effects. The amino acid tryptophan is also found in leafy green vegetables. It is a vital amino acid serving as a serotonin precursor. Serotonin is a neurotransmitter that produces a sound, cheerful mood.

Salmon

Salmon is one of the most nutritious and delicious foods available. It's high in protein and good for your skin. It benefits the eye and heart and even reduces weight. But one health advantage of eating salmon stands out above all others: brain health.

Sixty percent of the brain is fatty acids, the long snake-like fat molecules needed for brain development and function. Docosahexaenoic acid (DHA) makes up about two-thirds of brain fatty acids. It is like a warm winter coat for brain cells. You wouldn't leave home without a coat in the cold, so don't deprive your brain cells of DHA. This vital fatty acid protects neurons from damage, decreases brain inflammation, helps generate neurotransmitters, and is necessary for rapid information transmission along the axon, the neuron's highway. As we cannot produce these fatty acids, we must supplement our diet with them. Salmon is a very rich source of DHA.

Consuming salmon twice a week reduces memory impairments in adults aged 65 and over by 13%. Salmon also has vitamin D, which protects your skin from UV radiation. Seeing better skin in the mirror boosts your confidence and makes you happier, improving your mind and developing peace.

Turmeric

Turmeric, particularly its most active ingredient, curcumin, has several scientifically proven health advantages, including boosting heart health and preventing Alzheimer's disease and cancer. It also assists with depression and arthritic problems. Turmeric decreases inflammation while simultaneously increasing antioxidant levels. It supports your immune system while increasing oxygen intake in your brain, keeping you awake and ready to process information.

Before scientists' more significant knowledge of neurons, it was thought neurons couldn't split and proliferate after early development. However, now they know that this is not the case. Neurons can make new connections, increase and grow in number in particular brain parts. Brain-derived neurotrophic factor is one of the primary drivers of this process. The BDNF protein is involved in memory and learning. It is present in brain regions that control eating, drinking, and body weight. Many common brain illnesses, including depression and Alzheimer's disease, have been associated with decreasing BDNF protein levels. Curcumin, found in turmeric, can raise BDNF levels in the brain, promoting brain regeneration, memory, and learning.

Walnuts

If you have seen the picture of the brain, you are likely to compare walnuts with it. When you open the hard covering of a walnut, the soft part inside looks very similar to the brain. As described above, walnuts contain omega-3 fatty acids, which are beneficial for the brain.

Walnuts have the highest antioxidant activity than any other common nut. This effect is derived from melatonin, vitamin E, and plant substances known as polyphenols, which are abundant in the papery skin of walnuts. Walnuts also contain high quantities of zinc and magnesium, which are great for your mood, and being in a good mood is great for your brain performance.

Studies suggest that if your gut has a high concentration of health-promoting bacteria and other microorganisms, you are more likely to have a healthy gut and overall excellent health. What you consume has a big impact on the composition of your microbiota. Eating walnuts is one of the best methods to optimize your microbiome and gut health. An increase in bacteria that create butyrate, a lipid that nourishes your stomach and supports gut health, was among the results of eating walnuts.

High blood pressure is a significant risk factor for cardiovascular disease, brain damage, and stroke. Consuming walnuts can lead to a slight improvement in blood pressure. This is significant since even minor blood pressure variations are likely to influence your health significantly.

Dark Chocolate

Dark chocolate is a special delight on the list of foods for brain health for many people. Dark chocolate with a high cocoa content contains flavonoids. Flavonoids have been shown to enhance blood flow to the brain. Flavonoids may also help with memory and decrease cognitive deterioration.

The darker the chocolate, the more cocoa it contains. So, pick dark chocolate with at least 70% cocoa.

Dark chocolate is the most delicious brain enhancer. It includes a variety of natural stimulants, including theobromine, which improves attention and concentration while also stimulating the creation of endorphins, which improve mood. According to research, consuming dark chocolate can boost brain plasticity (the self-rewiring ability of the brain). Brain plasticity is important for learning and providing other brain-related advantages.

Chocolate includes tyramine, a crucial chemical generated from the amino acid tyrosine. Tyrosine is an amino acid that acts as a precursor to dopamine. Higher tyrosine levels result in increased dopamine levels, which activate the brain's reward center, improving your mood.

Half to one ounce of dark chocolate daily will give you all the benefits you need. This is one superfood where more is not necessarily better, so you must exercise caution with its consumption.

Coconut Oil

Many people praise coconut oil for its health advantages, which include antibacterial and antioxidant capabilities, enhanced skin and oral health, and the potential for weight loss.

Coconut oil includes medium-chain fats, which switch on your body's fat-burning furnace and aid in the production of ketones, feeding your brain. People have long utilized keto-diets, rich in fat and low in carbohydrates, to treat various illnesses, including drug-resistant epilepsy. They have been demonstrated to lessen the frequency of seizures. Coconut oil is also high in antioxidants, which assist in neutralizing potentially harmful chemicals known as free radicals. This, in turn, aids in the prevention of various chronic and degenerative disorders.

You need to be careful with coconut and not consume it excessively. An excellent way to consume it is to put it in mushroom coffee or a smoothie. You can also use it in place of butter, but do restrict your consumption to one teaspoon of coconut oil daily and not more.

Water

Last but certainly not least. Water should have been number one on this list, but I thought it would be better to discuss it here because it technically isn't food.

We need to stay hydrated. Sixty percent of our body is water, so maintaining this necessary substance is crucial in recovery. The body uses water to flush the kidneys, liver, intestines, or gut. Flushing and detoxification are very important in the case of drugs because the liver usually deals with their excretion, so water is needed to keep them healthy.

Moreover, water is good for your skin, hair, and nails. Although water doesn't provide energy, its deficiency can be a source of lethargy, and dehydration can also cause fatigue.

In recovery, there is no time to stop, no time to be slow. We need to keep on going and explore opportunities. We can't afford to be dehydrated. So, always drink plenty of water, at least 2-3 liters a day; the more, the better.

- -

Part 02: The Mind

-------------------------------- ---------

I have been talking about the mind from the start of this book because your mind is your most powerful tool. You can achieve anything if your mind is working in an ideal environment. So, your success must provide a winning environment for the mind.

Our mind works based on feelings and emotions. Daily, we come across multiple emotions; some are good, while others are bad. The bad emotions are full of negative energy. So they act like debris that clogs the cogwheels of your mind machinery. At the same time, good emotions clean the dirt and act as a lubricant to promote the optimum working of the mind. We must try to eliminate all these bad feelings and emotions and promote the good ones to keep our machinery of mind running efficiently.

The main focus of altering the environment of the mind includes altering the people you interact with, altering thoughts that feed into your mind, and changing your immediate environment. We will discuss all these things as we move on.

Altering the People That Surround You

The human brain is a fascinating and complex organ. It comprises neurons and the junctions between them, known as synapses. How your mind functions, thinks, and feels depends on the neurons and synapses. Although the number of neurons remains almost the same, the synapses between the neurons can change. So, we can change how our mind works. Studies have revealed that social interactions can impact our minds and alter synapses, showing that social interactions can affect how we think and feel.

People are constantly interacting with each other in some form or another. This can be through a conversation, a handshake, or even a glance. As people interact with one another, their brain waves sync up with each other. The more time two people spend interacting, the more attuned they become to each other's brain waves. This synchronization between two brains can be seen in how eye contact and facial expressions affect our brains. These interactions help us to process what someone else is saying and also have an effect on how we feel about them. There is a saying that "we are known by the company we keep." Others can identify us by looking at the people with whom we interact the most because our mind gets in sync with them.

There are advantages and disadvantages to the brain synchronization phenomenon. The advantage of brain syncing is that when we are depressed or stressed, we can easily change our condition by simply increasing our interaction with people who spread positivity and enjoy their life. Whereas suppose we start growing our interaction with negative people. In that case, we will be depleting our mental energy. Through the syncing process, we will alter our synapses to have negative thinking and feelings. So, to create a winning environment for the mind, we must surround ourselves with positive people.

Forming Barriers for Negative People

We interact with several people in our daily lives, and every person is somewhat different from the others. Some remain happy, have smiling faces, and enjoy their lives, while some are bombarded with problems. You might feel an aura of negativity around depressed people, but it is not strong enough to disrupt your positive energy. Your positive energy can help them by countering their negative energy.

However, the problem arises when you start interacting with negative people. These people have powerful negativity around them, which damages your mind.

Have you ever felt uncomfortable in the vicinity of a person? This happens because of the immense negative energy that they are expelling in the surroundings. When these negative people enter a room, they start sucking out the positive energy from your body, so it is very important to stay away from them. It would be best to minimize your time spent with individuals who drain your energy and don't add any value to your life.

This does not imply that you stop showing empathy for others. Put yourself in the shoes of others and live with compassion and empathy. Do all of this as part of being a good human being, but keep your life devoid of drama and negativity. Because it is not who you are. People in your life should be lessening your stress, not increasing it.

Staying Positive among Negative People

This concept is easy to understand but is very difficult to implement in your life because numerous people in our surroundings have some level of negativity. So it becomes near impossible to stay away from all of them. Moreover, certain people are important in your life, and you can't stay away from them. So, how can we counter this? We can counter this by staying positive among negative people.

The negative people are doing what they want, spreading negativity, and doing it excellently. The question is, are we, the positive people, doing our part correctly? Our task is simple, to stay positive, to spread positivity.

What happens in our life is that we get distracted from our path; we get affected by negativity and provide a place for it to fill. So, we need to start doing positive things, thinking positively, and feeling the positivity around us. We need to do things that make us happy and surround ourselves with people we enjoy. We need to chase our hobbies and perform positive affirmations.

Creating Winning Mentality

Now that we have abolished the negativity obstructing our minds, the next step is to empower our minds. We must train our minds toward love, abundance, and success. We need to create brain frequencies in the environment that attract positivity and abundance.

Preparation

The secret to every work and idea's success is its preparation. Without prior preparation, the task becomes challenging, and success seems impossible. Behind every successful project and event, numerous people prepared for it for several hours. The same is true for your mind's success. You must prepare your mind for winning.

When we sleep, our mind goes into a state where it shuts itself down and transfers all the data it had for the day to its hard drive. So, when you wake up, your mind is completely free and ready to accommodate anything you try to feed it. This is the best time for the preparation of your mind.

Our morning routine sets the tone for the rest of our day. Unfortunately, many of us now begin our days by checking our mobile phones. In the dark, we are drawn to the bright screen. We are hooked to these devices like a deer standing in the way of an incoming vehicle, hypnotized by staring at the lights. What a way to begin anything - with a habit that is harmful to our health!

Reading about another worldwide disaster or the death of a loved one is jarring to the brain. Given that news is mainly bad at all times, it's uncommon that any positive news or a nugget of important information comes in the early morning. It's like plunging into an ice lake in the dead of winter. Your breath is taken away by the cold. So, we should perform a positive activity instead of filling our minds with bad news.

The Three Tier Exercise

This is a 30-minute exercise that helps you prepare for the upcoming day early in the morning. It includes 10 minutes of reading great thoughts of other people, 10 minutes of reflecting on your thoughts, and 10 minutes of writing. This is a fairly simple exercise but can manifest awe-inspiring results.

Early in the morning, you stimulate your mind with positive thoughts by reading a book for 10 minutes. You can read books like a novel or a self-awareness book, anything that helps you grow and learn.

Next, it is time to reflect on your thoughts. Think of yourself as the boxer who clears his mind and devises a strategy before entering the ring. This is the time to clear your mind and think about what it will take for you to win today. Start by reflecting on what is important and what you can do today to bring you closer to your goal. Reflect on what you will do to align with your ultimate goal.

Finally, the 10 minutes allotted for writing can be spent brainstorming or writing a prompt. This is best done by hand. Handwriting has a physicality to it that helps warm up the intellect. It inspires a desire to own what appears on the paper. Today, it's too simple to click the erase key or edit. At the same time, we type on keyboards, forgetting what we've already written since AI often suggests the words. So, write anything with your hand that you think will help in the growth of your brain and will bring you a step closer to your goal. This simple yet effective exercise will create a positive winning environment for your mind early in the morning, and its effects will stay throughout the day.

Breaking It Down and Focusing

Now that you have prepared yourself, it's time to break down your journey into small steps. When we first begin our journey, our ultimate goal often seems challenging. This seeming difficulty causes us to procrastinate and demotivates us. The best way to keep your mind safe from an environment of procrastination is to break your journey into small steps. Achieving these small steps, one at a time, will boost our morale and help us create momentum. Breaking down your goal will boost your productivity and allow you to work on the details you might have missed.

Focusing on the task is important when you break down your goals. This will allow you to take your mind away from the ultimate goal and concentrate all of its energy on your smaller goals. The most efficient persons are productive not because they have a long list of tasks. In truth, it is because they understand how to concentrate on a certain activity without being distracted by anything.

How to breakdown goals

The best way to chunk down your goals is to set a time frame for achieving that goal. For example, you aim to eliminate bad habits in the next six months. Now, break down this goal into smaller milestones that you need to accomplish monthly. For example, if you decide to make your diet better for the first month, then you will start creating a winning environment for your mind in the next, and so on. Now the last step is to divide these milestones into actionable steps. Like you decide to start taking multivitamins from day one or cook salmon every Monday. Now that your goals have been broken down into smaller actionable steps; focus all your efforts on achieving your milestones one by one.

Another tip I would like to give you is to celebrate your wins. Celebrate every milestone, no matter how minor. It's important to remain focused on your goal to stay motivated through challenging times. But it's also vital to look back and celebrate how far you've already come, which boosts your mind.

Lion's Mindset

The lion is not frightened to pursue his desires. The lion is not scared to go his way while the others walk in the other direction; the lion is brave enough to protect and fight for his life. He lives his life exactly as he wishes.

When we refer to the lion mindset, the notion behind it is the fearlessness that it brings. A person with a lion mentality is driven to pursue and fulfil their life objectives. There is a greater emphasis on putting in the hard work and experiencing the outcomes rather than just wishing to go someplace. Individuals with a Lion mindset focus on their intentions and strive to overcome negativity or weaknesses. They have clear goals, and they keep on learning new skills necessary to achieve their goals. A lion's mindset is an excellent way of creating a winning mentality

How to Build Lion's Mindset

You should begin with simple measures when learning a lion mentality. Place a lion painting in your room, where you will see it daily to remind you of your goal. In addition, try incorporating the qualities of a person with a lion mentality into your daily life.

People who have a lion mindset are brave. They are fearless in standing up for what they believe. Even though they are terrified, they are ready to confront their opponents and their difficulties. Having a lion mindset starts with altering your perception of yourself. It grows when you have a positive attitude about yourself. It becomes stronger when you stop believing what people say about you. Write two affirmations and read them out loud to yourself daily to create positive thinking about yourself and develop the courage to face any challenge that comes your way.

People with a Lion Attitude are leadership symbols. They know exactly what they want. The lion, unlike the sheep, does not wait to be pushed about. He does not wait to be told what he can or cannot accomplish. He understands precisely what he wants and pursues it with all his resources.

If you wish to have the lion mindset, you must establish clear goals and work hard to achieve them. You should not trust what people say about your talents since a lion gets what he wants. Therefore, you should be prepared to go to any length to achieve your goals.

Senses

All the inputs into our minds come from our five senses: vision, hearing, taste, touch, and smell. Regulating all these senses is crucial to creating an optimum environment for our minds. Give extreme attention to what you are feeding your mind. Hearing negative comments, watching destructive movies, staying in an environment that stinks, tasting unhealthy food, and touching things filled with negativity can have immense adverse effects on your mind.

As discussed before, maintain a healthy diet. Develop the habit of listening to soothing music. Watch motivational videos and focus on constructive events. Cleanse your environment and add energizing scents to it. And keep things filled with positivity, like crystals, close to your body. So, keep your environment healthy and only give positive inputs to your mind so it enters efficient working mode

Neuroplasticity

Neuroplasticity, also known as neural plasticity, or brain plasticity, is the ability of neural networks in the brain to change through growth and reorganization. It is when the brain is rewired to function in some way that differs from how it previously functioned. Neuroplasticity allows the neurons in the brain to compensate for injury, addiction and disease and adjust their activities in response to new situations or changes in their environment.

Our brains are very adaptable to our surroundings. They will reallocate, prioritize, optimize, and move resources to weaker regions in need. People who have lost their eyesight have a more acute sense of hearing and touch. So, if, for some reason, one sense stops working, your brain rewires itself. The brain will heighten the other four senses to maximize your survival odds. Our brain is known for its efficiency, so it tends to strengthen those connections regularly used and eliminate those that haven't been used for a long time.

Our bad habits and cravings are the networks that need to be eliminated. So we must transduce the current from this network to other beneficial networks for the subsequent destruction of older pathways. Here I have listed some techniques to reprogram your brain and eliminate bad habits. The process of neuroplasticity requires time and repeatability, so ensure you perform these techniques regularly to attain maximum results.

New Language

Have you ever thought of learning a new language that fascinates you? Or there might be a language learning which can increase opportunities for you. Now might be the best time to fulfil this desire of yours. Language acquisition is a challenging but extremely rewarding task. In learning a new language, your brain forms many new neural pathways, so this practice is one of the best for rewiring your brain.

There is plenty of evidence that suggests that the process of learning a language improves cognitive function.

Your brain has two main parts, grey matter and white matter. Language acquisition has an advantageous effect on both these parts. Acquiring a new language has been shown to increase the density of your grey matter, which improves memory, attention, emotions, and motor skills and protects against cognitive decline. Language acquisition impacts the white matter by facilitating communication and connectivity between different brain parts. Many online apps help you acquire a new language, or you can enroll in a language class.

Music and Dance

Many world cultures consider music and dance as the language of the spirit. So, making music and learning new dance moves also has immense neuroplastic properties. Music and dancing can help improve mobility, coordination, and memory. However, it does more than merely assist in avoiding further cognitive impairment. It also aids in the relief of emotional discomfort and the enhancement of quality of life. It is never late to learn a new instrument or a new move. Multiple online resources can help you in learning, and you can even buy used instruments as well. So, explore your taste and start making music.

Video Games and Art

There has been a lot of controversy about the potential risks of video games. Still, numerous scientific studies have found that playing video games can alter the structure and functionality of your brain. Playing games improves motor learning, resilience, decision-making, reaction time, and cooperation. While playing different games, you train your brain to learn new skills. For example, puzzle games can teach you problem-solving.

The positive effects of playing games kick in after 16 hours of playtime, but you don't have to complete this all at once. I recommend adding two to three hours of gaming every week. Art also works like video games in enriching your brain's neural pathways.

Exercise

Exercise and workouts are recognized to provide multiple favorable effects, like stronger muscles, improved sleep, and better fitness. Exercise can help in neuroplasticity and offers numerous benefits to the brain. Exercise and workouts mainly target the skeletal muscles of our body. The skeletal muscles are very much like the brain cells. The brain cells or neurons can conduct voltages, as do the skeletal muscle cells. Hence muscle cells are part of your brain's wiring. So, exercising the muscles is a great way to strengthen neural networks and eliminate the bad ones.

Moreover, exercise increases blood flow to the brain, promotes cell growth, and repairs the brain. Exercising also stimulates the neurons to release various neurotransmitters into the blood. These neurotransmitters, including dopamine, serotonin, endorphins and epinephrine, alleviate your mood and bring joy. According to studies, aerobic exercises like rowing, running, cycling and swimming are most beneficial for changing the structure of the brain at the cellular level as well as the molecular level.

You'll undoubtedly get some social advantages too if you work out with someone else or in a bigger group. Strong social ties promote quality of life and emotional well-being. Thus, socializing with people daily could be an excellent method to improve brain wiring and alleviate anxiety symptoms. Exercise suggestions vary based on age, skill, and health, but exercising daily is a good idea.

Meditation

Meditation is one of the best, if not the best, ways to rearrange your brain networks. Although I will be discussing meditation in the next chapter in detail, I think it is vital to be included here because of its countless benefits to the brain. Meditation has different effects on certain brain parts. They all get summed up to rewire your brain into the best state possible.

Left Hippocampus

The left hippocampus is the brain region that ensures our learning. Cognitive ability, memory, emotional regulators, self-awareness, empathy, and gratitude are all related to the left hippocampus and its functionality. The functionality of the hippocampus is measured based on the volume of grey matter in the region. If the hippocampus has a lot of grey matter, the person will exhibit more cognitive and empathetic abilities. Meditation affects the hippocampus by thickening its grey matter. As a result, the meditator experiences an increase in cognitive ability, emotional regulation, self-awareness, and empathy, all of which are positive attributes.

Amygdala

Amygdala is an almond-shaped structure, mainly associated with emotions of fear, threat, stress, and anxiety. Similar to the hippocampus, its functionality lies in its grey matter region. However, the effect of meditation is different in this structure. Meditating regularly causes the thinning of the grey matter amygdala. As your amygdala shrinks, you feel less anxious and stressed.

Posterior Cingulate

The posterior cingulate is responsible for your wandering thoughts and sense of self. The larger the posterior cingulate, the more capable the person can stay focused and having a realistic notion of the self. Meditation increases the volume of the posterior cingulate, making it more functional. This results in enhanced concentration and a more fine-tuned sense of self. This fine-tuned sense of self is extremely important when talking about the mind since the mind is responsible for understanding and projecting the self.

Without the mind, you would not have an understanding of yourself. Since meditation increases this part of the brain that regulates the self, meditation can allow your mind to more clearly conceive of yourself and your place in this world.

Temporo Parietal Junction (TPJ)

The TPJ is the part of the brain that allows us to be empathetic and compassionate. It is associated with our sense of perception, which often makes us more compassionate and empathetic. When we put ourselves in another person's shoes, the TPJ becomes active. Meditation increases the volume of the TPJ. Increasing the volume of TPJ allows us to become better people and achieve certain personal goals we set for ourselves. As a result, meditation allows us to take the image we have for ourselves and turn it into reality.

Creating a winning environment for the mind means you should positively surround your mind. Formulate hobbies that bring positivity to your life. Think about the ways to be positive. Eliminate all negative thoughts from your mind and divert all your focus to achieving your goal. Get rid of fear and uncertainty and develop clear intentions. There is nothing you can't achieve, so keep your mind prepared for your success.

Summary

How your mind functions, thinks, and feels depends on the neurons and synapses. The main focus of altering the environment of the mind includes altering the people you interact with and the thoughts that feed into your mind. As people interact and their brains sync, they become more attuned to each other. The advantage of brain syncing is that when we are depressed or stressed, we can easily change our condition by increasing our interaction with positive people.

People in your life should be lessening your stress, not increasing it. If you focus your attention and energy on negative individuals and negativity, their breath will infiltrate your existence. Don't let them drain your energy; concentrate on what is good, and you will attract more good. We must train our minds toward love, abundance, and success.

One way to develop a winning environment is to be prepared for success. When we sleep, our mind goes into a state where it shuts itself down. It is the best time to prepare our minds when we wake up. This is the time to clear your mind and think about what it will take for you to win and prepare yourself for it.

Breaking down the journey into small steps helps concentrate the mind's energy. Achieving these small steps, one at a time, will boost morale and help create momentum. The most efficient persons are productive not because they have a long list of tasks but because they understand how to concentrate on a certain activity without being distracted.

Another excellent way to create a winning environment is to have a lion's mindset. A person with a lion mentality is driven to pursue and fulfil their life objectives. Having a lion mindset starts with altering your perception of yourself. It becomes stronger when you stop believing what people say about you.

Neuroplasticity is the ability of neural networks in the brain to change through growth and reorganization. It is when the brain is rewired to function in some way that differs from how it previously functioned. Our brains adapt to our surroundings and reallocate, prioritize, optimize, and move resources to the needed regions. Performing certain repetitive tasks will allow you to rewire your mind and transfer energy away from the bad neural links, weakening them and ultimately eliminating them. Learning a new language, making music, playing video games, and exercising is great for rearranging neural synapses. Meditation is also highly beneficial for this purpose. The positive effects it provides to the brain are as complex as the brain itself.

Creating a winning environment for the mind means you should positively surround your mind. All the inputs that go into our minds come from our five senses. So, put positivity in all your input and develop an environment where your mind flourishes.

Part 03: The Spirit

We have reached our ultimate goal. I have been talking about the power of our body, mind, manifestation, and vibrations. Still, I haven't properly introduced you to the source of these powers. The source of our powers and our existence comes from our spirits. The energy for everything we think and perform comes from our spirit. You have probably heard of the word "spirit" before but are unlikely to have properly understood it. In this chapter, I will introduce you to your ultimate energy source. I will be directing you to create the most optimal environment for this source to operate at its peak and provide you with what you truly desire.

What is Spirit?

Spirit is a concept that is unique to every person. So everyone will have their explanation and definition of spirit. For me, the spirit is a never-ending, unseen force that dwells within every person and all other worldly things. It is the driving force that contributed to the creation of everything on this earth. It is the energy that brings everything into manifestation. Spirit is the center of your existence and the source of all your knowledge. It is the part of you that knows everything about this universe. The voice inside your head that guides you into believing what is wrong and right is the spirit.

Spirit is the pathway that links you to everything in this universe. You can understand spirit as the core energy of this universe, and you have the tiniest part of this power inside you as well.

You might have understood something about the spirit from what I discussed above if you reverse your mind and remember the vortex chapter. I discussed that you need to enter the vortex to recover from your bad habits and gain success. Inside the vortex, your energy will get unified with the energy of this universe, and whatever you desire will manifest automatically. Well, the spirit is that energy.

You should understand that spirit is more important than your body and mind. So, you need to create a winning environment for your spirit. You might think that if the spirit is most important, why am I talking about it in the end? Because you can't create a winning environment for your spirit without caring for your body and mind. You can't keep your spirit healthy if your body and mind are unhealthy.

Spiritual Meditation

As you may know, meditation is great resource humans have discovered across history and in different cultures. It is profoundly therapeutic to quiet the mind, relax the soul, and become more present at the moment. Even folks who're not religious have discovered that turning down the volume has an advantage.

The process of creating the perfect environment for your spirit is meditation. Meditation is at the top of the list of almost every spiritual healer or holistic health worker. It is also the number one choice when it comes to spiritual awakening. There are many types of meditation, but as depicted by its name, spiritual meditation is the most beneficial for your spirit.

What is Spiritual Meditation?

Spiritual meditation is a technique in which you participate to communicate with a higher authority, the Universe, or your Higher Self. Unlike other types of meditation, spiritual meditation is more than just stress relief or relaxation. The desire to connect with something greater than oneself distinguishes this activity as spiritual. It is a profound personal experience that might seem significantly different for each individual.

Spiritual experiences may include the following characteristics: evaporation or elimination of a sensation of separateness, experiencing a spiritual connection, and feeling of transcendence to a higher place. You should not attempt to impose an intuitive link to something more profound, whether you feel it or not. If you are new to spiritual meditation, avoid interactions in which others discuss their spiritual meditation practice experiences. This can help to avoid having unreasonable ideas about what your practice should feel like. Since we are all incredibly distinct people, everybody's experiences will be distinctive.

Benefits of Spiritual Meditation

Spiritual meditation promotes a more balanced state of being, inner serenity, and tranquility. It inspires you to accomplish everything with intent. When you meditate regularly, you can more accurately pay attention to what your body desires. Spiritual meditation provides a true feeling of who you are. It improves creativity and offers clarity to your life's purpose. It does everything to enhance the growth of your spirit. However, the benefits it brings come from dedication to daily practice and the willingness to grow.

How to Perform Spiritual Meditation

Similar to every meditation, this one also starts with sitting comfortably in a calm and silent environment. Using a pillow to sit on is recommended as it is more comfortable. Now, put your right hand on the center of the heart, and your left hand goes to just under the belly button. Maintain an upright posture. Breathe slowly and deeply.

Listen to your breath and start to connect with it. Listen to the sound of your breath and feel this sound as your body moves. Now observe the rhythm of your breathing. Allow your consciousness to tune into your heart rate as you get more tuned in to your breathing. Feel the beats of your heart. It's completely fine if your mind wanders. Applaud your consciousness and bring back your focus from distractions. Allow your consciousness to travel into your heart and observe how you feel there.

Now visualize a light inside you. Pour the brightness and color into it and feel its warmth. This light is the energy inside you. Now visualize this light getting out of your body and connecting with everything surrounding you. Feel the energy that this light is pouring into your body and mind. Now, slowly make this light return to the core of your body. Open your eyes and move slowly as you come out of meditation.

When to Perform Meditation

You can meditate at any time of the day. However, it is believed that your body is more open to giving and receiving in the morning and evening. So, meditating at this time will yield the most jarring results.

Suppose you decide to perform meditation early in the morning. In that case, it is suggested that you journal or do the 10-minute exercise described in the previous chapter to clear your mind about what is coming. In meditation at night, put your phone on do not disturb mode. Leave it like this until the morning. For an exceptionally peaceful sleep, limit your screen time once you have finished meditation and go straight to bed.

It doesn't matter whether you do it in the morning or evening. The thing that matters is the intention. So, set your positive intentions before you start meditation at any time of the day or night.

Gratitude

Practicing gratitude comes right after spiritual meditation because of its role in love. Adding additional gratitude to your life can transform it. The more thankful you get and practice gratitude, the more will be provided to you for what you're grateful for by the universe. Gratitude profoundly affects the spirit, so it is considered one of the best practices for creating a winning environment.

What is Gratitude?

Gratitude is derived from the Latin word gratus, which means "pleasant; welcoming; nice." Gratus is also the basis of words like grace, gratuity, and gratis, which all refer to pleasant emotions, deeds, and concepts. This is due to the Proto-Indo-European root gwere, which means "to laud, to rejoice; to be in touch with the Divine." In other words, sensing the presence of the higher self in

our life is similar to gratitude. It is equivalent to being in a state of happiness. It enables us to perceive the worth, virtue, and usefulness of everything. In this way, gratitude can be considered an antidote to many types of suffering, including bad habits.

There are two stages of gratitude. The first stage is to identify the good in one's life. When we are grateful, we declare that our life is wonderful and full of aspects that make it worthwhile to live. Our life is beautiful. The recognition that we have attained something is pleasing to us because of its existence and the work and effort we have put in to attain it.

You reach the second stage of gratitude when you acknowledge that not all of the goodness in your life comes from within you or from the things you have. Some source of this beauty of your life is external. When you reach this stage, you realize that you must be grateful to the environment, the people, and the living beings around you. Your life is vastly affected by your surroundings. Arriving at this stage sends you on a discovery spree to spread gratitude for every factor that has brought pleasure to your life.

In short, these two stages of gratitude are the awareness of the happiness in our life and the elaboration of how this happiness got to us.

Benefits of Gratitude

One emotion that obstructs the energy flow of our spirits is jealousy, and gratitude is the easiest way to suppress this emotion. When you feel thankful, you have no space in your head for negative emotions such as fear, wrath, or envy. You are aware that you are living in total wealth. You are aware that you have all you need. And you are aware that you influence your happiness. What others have has no bearing on how you perceive your own life.

The most beneficial advantage of gratitude is the development of love. Gratitude is the source of developing self-love as well as love for others. When you practice gratitude, you focus on the positive aspects of your personality. So in the first stage of gratitude, you develop a love for yourself. You acknowledge that your steps have brought serenity to your life. As you reach the second stage of gratitude, you start feeling love for everything this universe has. This happens because you know that every piece of this universe contributes to your life's happiness.

Now, why is this love important for us to attain success in our goals? Nature is kept together by the energy of love, and actions inspired by love need the least effort. You squander energy when you want power or money. In contrast, when your activities are driven by love, your energy expands, and the surplus energy is channeled into manifesting what you want.

Gratitude can help us become more linked with the universe and the core of the spirit. It gives us a new perspective on our lives, helping us see the good in every circumstance and understand that life happens for us, not to us. It awakens a higher awareness, allowing us to form a profound connection with the cosmos.

How to Practice Gratitude

Practicing gratitude is as easy as opening your lips and speaking words. There are many ways to practice gratitude; these are simple and easy.

Notice Good Things in Your Life

Begin to observe and recognize the things for which you are grateful. Pay attention to the small details of your daily life and observe the nice things you may take for granted.

One way of noticing good things in your life is to analyze your life and think of three things you are grateful for. This practice needs to be repeated daily. It's surprising what you notice when you concentrate on being thankful. Writing is a powerful way of stimulating your mind and spirit, so writing these things in a journal is an excellent practice.

You can also incorporate some other things in your journal. This can include answers to questions like, what inspiration did I get today, and from what? Which thing brought peace in my life today? And what actions have enhanced my happiness today?

As you write in your journal, try not to repeat anything from your previous days. This will enable you to look more deeply inside yourself and focus on the small details of your day which make you happy. It could be a bite of your favorite food, a call from a friend, an aroma you might have experienced while passing by a flower shop, or a scene from a movie that brought a smile to your face. Focusing on these little things will amplify your feelings of gratitude exponentially.

You can write your journal before bedtime, early morning, or before or after meditation. The time of the day doesn't matter. What matters is that you intentionally take a few minutes from your day to analyze and observe your life. Look back on things that have contributed to the happiness in your life. Commit to maintaining the diary for a month.

What we focus on increases in our lives. So, practicing gratitude is a sure way of bringing more and more blessings into your life.

Keep an Eye on Your Future

It's easy to start seeing the glass as half-empty rather than half-full, so one strategy is to seek things to be grateful for before they happen. There is a lot in this world that is fantastic, and it's simple to locate those things. This allows you to be on the lookout for good continually. It would be best if you considered possible future actions for which you can be grateful. These actions could be the ones that bring happiness to your life or another. For example, you might find out that buying a cup of coffee today will bring joy to your life, so be grateful for this action before you even perform it. You might have promised your friend you would help them with a project or task. So, be grateful that you are about to spread happiness in someone's life. By thinking about your possible actions for which you should be grateful, you start taking more and more steps towards gratitude. Your daily life gets filled up with numerous actions for which you show gratitude.

Express Gratitude

Gratitude is more than etiquette, manners, or politeness. It's about expressing your honest emotions of thankfulness. When you thank someone, you also exercise the first two gratitude skills: you have observed something nice and appreciated it.

There are many ways through which you can express gratitude. One way is to show appreciation to people who have done something nice to you or brought happiness to your life.

Write Gratitude Letter

Make a list of five persons who have significantly affected your life. Pick one and compose a thank-you note to convey your appreciation for all the presents you've received from that individual. Deliver your thanks note in person if feasible.

While we often express our gratitude orally, the written word is sometimes more impactful since someone took the time to pen down their thanks. A letter may also be re-read and loved, causing joy and love to spread across the globe.

Do Kindness

Gratitude can motivate you to repay a favor or to behave with compassion or kindness. Or you could come upon a circumstance where you can pay it forward. Small acts of kindness include gestures like keeping the door open for someone who once did something good for you. Even if you have to wait longer than usual, you can perform someone else's duties without revealing who you are. Take note of how you feel afterward.

Walk for Gratitude

This is a very beneficial exercise when feeling low or stressed out. Set out at least 20 minutes to walk around your neighborhood, in a park, near your workplace, or anywhere in nature.

Consider how thankful you are for loving relationships, financial comforts, the body that enables you to see the world, the intellect that allows you to comprehend yourself, and your core spiritual essence while you walk. Breathe, stop, and be thankful for the air that fills your lungs and allows you to live.

Pay attention to everything you see, hear, feel, smell, and maybe even taste, and observe how many things you can discover to be thankful for. This is an excellent method to transform your attitude and open yourself to the flow of abundance that constantly surrounds you.

Spiritual Fellowship

You all have heard about unity and are likely to know its importance. Spiritual fellowship is all about unity. Teamwork or unity is crucial factor in an organization or any project. When one person tries to complete everything, he most likely fails. Similarly, if all the team members are hardworking but don't have harmony, they are most likely bound to fail. Even if they succeed, they may take more time than those with unity. This happens because when people work or try to achieve a similar goal with unity, they fill up the shortcomings of their fellows, and so they grow and succeed together. This unity also has positive effects on the aspects of the spirit.

The Spiritual Fellowship brings together a group of like-minded spiritually awakened or awakening people who have the same goals and work together to accomplish everything. Spiritual fellowship is founded on fundamental ideas. Few spirits on this planet survive in perfect isolation from one another; they should not. Therefore, we need one another as mirrors for development and transformation. When two or more individuals are nearby, they share magnetic vibrations. So, whether positive or negative, this greater magnetism typically takes precedence.

The great saints have such enormous attraction that their presence can affect the people around them. As for the rest, we must be careful who we spend our time with since the people in our life are the most crucial component of our surroundings. So, to create a winning environment for your spirit, you need to fellowship with people who have achieved similar goals or are trying to achieve a similar purpose. Because in this way, your energies will get combined and amplified, allowing you to face success sooner.

If you try to find people with which you can practice spiritual fellowship and fail, you don't need to worry about it. As I have described before, you are never alone in this world. This universe and your higher self are always nearby, so feel the whole universe's presence with you and become close to nature because the universe is all about nature.

Spirit and Nature

Nature can instill spiritual strength and relevance. Nature often evokes a sense of divine awe. Prana, the primal life energy that nourishes all life, is abundant in nature. So it immerses you in the whirling currents of prana as it circulates and flows throughout nature.

The connection to spirit is far more profound than in urban or contained places. This is because the natural world embodies attributes of the flow state. You come into direct touch with pure creativity, happiness, development, and action while you are in nature. So, by being in nature, you embody all these spirit traits at your deepest level. This is why spending time in nature is the most effective approach to reconnecting with the universe. With each thought, the plants' aroma enters your lungs, the waters of tides stream through your blood, and the energy of a lightning storm shines through your head. All this forms your union with the universe. So, spending at least one day close to nature and meditating during this time can further boost the effects.

Forgiveness

Forgiving and asking for forgiveness are the most crucial parts of spiritual progress. There is more to forgiveness than saying, "I forgive you" or "I apologize." It is a feeling deep inside you, and when forgiveness happens, the spirit undergoes profound transformations.

When we forgive someone, we heal ourselves and reduce our karmic load. It not only removes the harm and agony inflicted by the other but also extinguishes the previous damage. It no longer obstructs our spiritual progress and hastens a fresh beginning with that individual. It cleanses the negativity that would otherwise eat away our vitals and interfere with our thinking process.

There are two types of forgiveness, both of which are interconnected. Self-forgiveness allows us to let go of our shame and pride. Then there is the forgiveness we offer and receive from others, both friends and foes. Both are equally important, so practicing both creates the optimum environment for your spirit.

How to Practice

As writing amplifies the stimulation of mind and spirit, this practice also includes writing. Take a piece of paper and pen and write about your guilt. Write about the things you haven't forgiven yourself for. Similarly, write the things you haven't forgiven others on another paper. Now, take one thing at a time from the list and practice forgiveness. The best for this is again writing. You can write letters to yourself and others to express your feelings about the event and to forgive.

Another practice concurrently with this one is asking other people for forgiveness. Ask others verbally or through letters for forgiveness. Do this with everyone close to you. Even if you don't know about anything happening for which you ask for forgiveness, write or say, "If I have ever done wrong to you, please forgive me."

There are many other practices that you can do to create a winning environment for your spirit. These include practicing patience, spreading kindness, being truthful, being open to new experiences, and finding something to believe. Keep swapping your body, mind, and spirit environment from the clutter and fill your life with happiness and tranquility.

Summary

Spirit is a never-ending, unseen force that dwells within every person and all other worldly things. It is the driving force contributing to the creation of everything on earth. You can understand spirit as the core energy of this universe, and you have the tiniest part of this power inside you as well. So, you need to create a winning environment for your spirit.

Spiritual meditation is a technique in which you participate to communicate with a higher authority, the Universe, or your Higher Self. There are many types of meditation, but as depicted by its name, spiritual meditation is the most beneficial for your spirit.

Gratitude profoundly affects the spirit, so it is considered one of the best practices for creating a winning environment. Gratitude is the source of developing self-love as well as love for others. One way of noticing good things in your life is to analyze your life and think of three things you are grateful for. It's surprising what you notice when you concentrate on being thankful.

Writing and asking other people for forgiveness are two imssportant practices to create the optimum environment for your spirit. Practice patience, spreading kindness, being truthful, being open to new experiences, and finding something to believe.

Conclusion/Final Thoughts

Starting this chapter, I congratulate you on being consistent and developing the courage to embrace inner change. In this final chapter, I will conclude all of our book discussions. Moreover, I will be talking a bit about my thoughts and lifestyle. You will get a sneak peek into how you can incorporate everything written in this book into your life. So, let's cherish our final few moments to learn something incredibly beneficial.

The inspiration behind this book is not just to help people with bad habits. It is to let them understand that they are not victims of their circumstances but rather architects of their lives. Everyone has tragedies, obstacles, and roadblocks in life. That is the simple truth of life. Nobody ever promised that life would be easy. Although we have no control over where or under what circumstances we are born, we have power over everything that happens after that.

We are where we are due to our choices and decisions. And so, we do have the ability to shape our future and present. You are self-sufficient; you have everything needed to be a better person. All you need to do is discover your true inner power. Healing is possible. I don't care which caste, creed, religion, or color you belong to; you can take charge of your life now and start moving ahead.

My goal was to create a step-by-step bible for recovery and how people can become the best possible version of themselves. Although the environment is crucial in developing our habits for good or worst, some aspects of our personality can also tangent us towards bad habits.

And so it is vital that through the recovery process, we work on ourselves and emerge as transformed beings.

The first step in every journey is realizing that the journey is required in the first place. And then believing everything is possible and that we can escape our misery. Believing in yourself is the foundation of transformation. For everything else to work out, first, you must believe. Many people fail to diverge from bad habits because they lack belief in themselves. I started this book, the journey to your transformation, by making you believe in yourself through an insight into the power of the mind and imagination that has always been inside us.

Every working body has some laws and principles, including this universe. Therefore, knowing the laws of this universe that have governed us since the first human appeared in this universe is essential in maintaining optimum navigation in our daily lives. These laws provide the power of manifestation to every human being, so learning to manifest within these laws uplifts us to the rank of the creator. Being the creator is an advantage only given to those who produce awareness. However, being aware and manifesting is not that simple. We must be ALIGNED WITH NATURE. We must have a clear personal purpose and passion and constantly pursue it.

Adjusting our vibration in comparison to the higher self is the only way to tap into the vortex and become singular with the source. However, learning to adjust our vibrations could also be detrimental to prosperity. So, learning to take in light in a way that allows us to shine is the key to life. Learning to program what I call THE CPU OF THE GODS will raise our frequencies to that of our heart's desires. Cultivating our gardens, the garden of our mind, body, and spirit, will guarantee the best outcomes.

Everything in this universe works in a cycle; therefore, you can't reach your goal in one go. You can only reach there by going through the cycle of efforts repeatedly. It's only this repeated cycle that will elevate us. The more we repeat it, the easier it will become, and the easier we will be elevated. We need to be consistent in the repetition of this cycle. Because without being consistent until we reach our goals, we will fail.

Now the question is, what is this cycle all about? This cycle is about creating a winning environment for our body, mind, and spirit. What we put into the earth (our bodies) and what we feed it determines the growth and frequency of the final product. The final matter is determined and developed by the elements that are its ingredients. Hence, when we put the elements of a healthy body, mind, and spirit in our diet, we manifest a recovered and healthy being. Therefore, learn to take in carefully and give out only what is of good reward and worthy of the gods.

You need to remember throughout this cycle that the craving or the urges will come. You can't just take a decision and be done with it. Making the decision will change the trajectory of your mind, but for your body to change the course, it takes time. So, whenever you drive past a bar or a club, that smell and magnetism will attract your body. During your low time, this magnetic field will try to engulf you. But, you need to become impeccable and win over these urges.

Being IMPECCABLE is a process that takes a large amount of DISCIPLINE to achieve regardless of the know-how. Being able to control emotions and bad cravings and do what is needed, regardless of the sacrifice or difficulty, separates those who can achieve from those who cannot. Knowledge is the only thing that helps you to become impeccable, and it is only powerful when applied correctly. So, acquire knowledge about life, and use it correctly. Be a master and a student of your life at the same time.

We have gone over many laws, principles, and methods to free our minds of bad habits. However, we can have all the knowledge in the world yet no power. Applying that knowledge and the will to persist will give us the power we desire. To reach the Promised Land, we must keep moving forward. BACKWARDS IS NOT AN OPTION. Therefore, brief or simple persistence is the key that opens all doors.

My life has been one of chaos and achievements, joy and pain. Balancing life's scale and doing what's needed to manifest one's goals takes extreme tenacity and resilience to which there is no compromise. There is a deadline on when to get focused; however, the date is underdetermined, so the sooner, the better.

An Ideal Day

As you read the book, I have shared various advice and techniques to help you improve your lifestyle to benefit your accelerated recovery. However, you might have gotten overwhelmed by all the things. You might be wondering how you incorporate these into your own lifestyle. So, I have decided to share my life routine with you to give a practical example of everything I have discussed.

An ideal day would be waking up early, around 5 am. I do my morning meditation at this time, as early morning is one of the best times to perform meditation. At this particular time of the day, there is silence and calm everywhere, so you don't have difficulty focusing. An important thing to note here is that, contrary to the usual trend, I don't check my phone or TV because I don't want to fill my head with worries at this time of blessing.

I like to play music in the background because it helps me focus. So, before meditating, I turn on some serene, soothing binaural beat frequency music. I take three to five deep breaths from the diaphragm, centering my mind and body. Then I close my mind and focus on LOVE and ABUNDANCE as my mind drifts off. I continue focusing for the next 10 - 20 minutes. Then, when I am ready, I slowly bring my attention back to my body and open my eyes.

Meditating has ignited my mind, and it's time to stimulate the body. So, the next step is to get up and perform stretching exercises for 20 minutes. Then I relax my body for a while and go to the shower.

Now comes the step of preparing my diet and filling my body with healthy ingredients. I usually prepare a fully nutritious smoothie of 2 fruits and a vegetable (Blueberries, Banana, apple, and ginger or spinach). As I do all this, I prepare my body and mind for the upcoming greatness that will unfold today.

Then I go off to work, and during the whole day, I keep repeating the laws and principles of the universe in my mind and try to benefit from them whenever I see the chance. This part is usually different every day, so I mold myself accordingly.

After work, I hit the gym for 30 minutes to one hour. Exercise is always good for your body, but you can list this time as your hobby. I go to the gym because I like to work out and keep my body fit. It is my hobby.

My supper consists of a salad full of green leafy vegetables. I read afterward and cleaned my bed for a night of deep sleep.

I prepare my LOVE and ABUNDANCE frequency to play while I sleep, so I meditate before bed. And then, it's Good Night, giving my body and mind the rest for the next great day.

My daily routine is just an example for you. Because everyone has a unique way of living, you can modify your schedule according to your needs.

In this book, I have tried to introduce you to the Quantum Side of addiction and provide you with practical techniques to recover. I have tried to give you all the vital knowledge you need to modify your life to create the optimum recovery environment

As I have been through all this, I know that it will take some time before you find the right way in your life. I hope my words have been helpful to you and you form a connection to the source of this universe's energy. I wish you tap into your higher self and encounter a life filled with LOVE and ABUNDANCE.

Bonus: Edges of Ability

So you've got this new mindset. So you've graduated, and no longer are you the same person you used to be. You've changed. You've learned what it takes to be the person you need to be to get where you want to go. And you're ready. You've put in the work. You've cried some nights and laughed a others. In your mind, you've gotten through the most challenging part. You broke the chains of bad habits. You've transformed your minds from busted and disgusted into believed and achieved. And the road ahead is paved with infinite possibilities and potential. It's possible.

We learn new things in life daily. We test what we learn all the time. Win, lose or draw, the strong and resilient grow regardless.

A strong person knows that the goal, regardless of failure, is to keep the vision and stay the course, regardless of how prepared I am. To grow and advance, I have to live on the edges of my ability.

A lawyer doesn't attend law school for three to five years, graduate, pass the bar, and start a career as a painter. No, his journey has just begun. Now it's time to stand in court. Now it's time to test all the years of school. Now it's time to stand before a judge and try his case. A doctor doesn't attend Med School for an average of ten years, graduates, and becomes a bus driver. No, it's time to operate. It's time to perform surgeries and save lives. It's time to make it all add up.

A boxer or UFC fighter trains day in and day out. His focus, while he trains, is on one day, his next fight. Every day of training, he breaks his last day's record. He bends the bow. He pushes the mark. He raises the bar. He has the discipline to push past the pain and stay the course for one day. All the pain, blood, sweat, and tears will be tested. He knows leaving it all in the ring is more important than winning.

If he loses after he gives it his all, he is back to the drawing board with new insight, a stronger belief, and an act of new courage. But if he doesn't give it his all, if he chokes and doesn't loosen up and let the punches flow, he loses with a world of regret. His will is shot. His drive is gone, and his mind is now his biggest enemy, his biggest critic. It was all a waste.

All the blood, sweat, tears, time, and pain put into a win is now time wasted on a loss—a loss in time, a waste of effort and skill. A give up. It takes courage to test your abilities. If you're truly exhausted from being sick and tired, get courage. Get the courage to go completely the other way.

It takes courage not to answer the phone when those old deadbeat friends keep calling. It takes courage to have a new mindset and to go into new ways of living. It takes courage to fight the urges. It takes courage to shake the Devil off and off and off again. Did I say it takes courage to fight the urges?

It takes courage to have discipline. It takes courage to get out of the rut comfort zone and plant yourself in a better one. It takes courage to leave behind a bad lover or family member. It takes courage not to give in to the quick flashes.

It takes courage to stop walking and start running. It takes courage to get out of the prison of your mind and grow. It takes courage to jump off the cliff, the cliff of poverty and pity, into power and passion. You can't plant a seed of hope in the small soils of addiction and temporary fixes. You can't expect to grow big dreams in small minds.

Stop looking for someone to pat you on your back. Stop walking along slowly, waiting for it to fall in your lap. You got to run after your destiny. Pick up the pace.

Success isn't an accident. It's a passionate pursuit. Success isn't a one-time effort. Success is leaving it all in the ring. Success is not about what others think. Success is living life on the brink. Success isn't about, well, I don't feel like it today. Success is about I'm going to do it anyway. Success never says I'm afraid of how it all might go.

Let me say a quote from Ben Franklin. He said, "the thinking I have now has created problems. This mindset, this thinking cannot solve. No doubt we are not the same person we were when we started this, correct? It's safe to say our thinking has changed a bit." Correct.

When we learn a new language, the best way to develop it is to use it as often as possible, my brothers and sisters. Now is the time. Now is the time to test the theories. Now is the time to apply the skills and techniques. Now is the time to do new things. Now is the time to pick up the pace. Now is the time to have the audacity to be better, to do better.

Nothing changes until our energy changes. But here's the catch. You see, the energy never rests. It either goes forward, or it goes backward. It never rests. So if we are not moving forward, learning new things, developing new connections, exploring new heights, and taking new risks that will raise us, if we are not doing these things, it's safe to say our energy has nothing to grab on to, to accept our past histories. It's safe to say we have to develop new memories because the old ones created problems that are no longer Vibing Coherently With Who I Am, Who We Are, and the new me. Now, Stop Splitting Your Energy.

We manifest when Energy is steadily moving forward. Let me share something with you. Now it's time. Now it's the time to live on the edge of the new you. Push this person to new heights and new directions. Live on The Edge Of Your Abilities.

When we do this, when we live this way, we grow. When we abandon bad memories of what led us down bad pathways, when we do, we develop new patterns in our brains. When we do this, we start to unravel the tightly fused knot. Be grateful, my friends; we made it out alive. Many were not lucky enough. My friends, we were granted a second chance, and some of us got a third or fourth chance to live again. Be grateful, my friends. We still have sand left in our hourglass.

Be grateful, my friends, because the truth is that it could have been you. It could have been me. Get off your ass and take advantage of it. Please do yourself a big favor, do it now, and stop delaying. The best way to predict the future is to create it yourself.

Do yourself a favor, stop getting in where you don't fit, and get in where you belong.

Do yourself a favor and act as if there's no limit to your abilities. Assume the best outcome in everything. Practice being successful. Don't worry about how crazy you sound to others. George Bernard Shaw said, "The reasonable man bends and adapts to the ways and demands of the world. The unreasonable man persists in trying to adapt the world to himself. Therefore, all progress depends on the unreasonable man".

Joe Frank says. "A Soft, Feeble, Frail Fellow Does What He Thinks Pleases Others To Get By. A Strong, Confident, Assertive Person Does What He Feels, What He Is Called To Do, Regardless Of Opinions. Therefore, Success Is Built On The Shoulders Of The Assertive Man." Let me drop a gem on you; you might want to write it down, "Release the Thinking of Not Wanting to Accept New Information Because It Doesn't Sound right."

Do yourself a favor and stop resisting what feels new and uncomfortable. Learn to accept, change, and grow. Learn how to give up the fear of looking stupid because you don't understand or learn as fast as others. Do you want not to know and stay broke or look stupid while you're rich?

Every day when we rise is a test day. We either pass or fail. So, learn to push, pull, pinch, or bite. We never lose the fight when we live on The Edge of Our Abilities. Never Lose The Fight.

Resources

(*YouTube Channel* -----"The Quantum Side of Addiction")

To all those who have helped me in any way along the way:

Just know you have a confidante and friend. As life turns, the pendulum swings; this is inevitable. True self-mastery begins when we manipulate and conjure the natural universal forces given to us all. We will cross paths again, and may the LOVE AND ABUNDANCE in me have overtaken you till we meet again. May all your dreams enter into the VORTEX... In THE QUANTUM SIDE.

Special Thanks

Helping Up Mission
1029 E Baltimore St, Baltimore, MD 21202
410.929.6999 - 410.675.4357(m)
410.675.7500
philanthropy@helpingup.org
www.helpingupp.org

Powell Recovery Center14 S Broadway, Baltimore, MD 21231, United States
410.276.1773
www.prcinc.org

Tinia Massenburg
Womens Recovery Housing
Time Organization
443.416.0298

Kenneth Bass
Mens Homeless Shelter
Time Organization
1211 N. Chester Street (410.801.6622)

Hel Recovery Center
1900 N. Howard St. Baltimore, MD 21219
443.869.5393
referrals@helwellness.com

Kelley Meyers
Maryland Recovery Homes
443.431.3802

Josh Shetterly
Peer Recovery Space
Franklin Square
443.632.5433

Diana
One Voice Methadoxe Clinic
410.402.4078

Tuerk House
Maryland Crisis Stabilization Center
2701 North Charles Street, 21218
676.212.2631

Recovery Network
21W. 25th St. Baltimore MD 21218
410.366.1717 (p) 410.889.4167 (f)
www.recoverynetwork.org

Molly Majors
Recovery Centers of America
Via Facebook

Jason
One Promise Treatment Center
443.469.9373

Richard
Maryland Health Department
443.858.2792

Pricilla
Peace Healthcare
410.499.4707

Behavioral Health Services
443.242.6535
INFO4Refine@gmail.com

Glenwood Life Counseling Center
410.323.9811, ext.242
awinepol@glenwoodlife.org

University Psychological Center, Inc.
6201 Greenbelt Road Suite U-3. College Park MD 20740
301.345.1919 (p)
301.345.5779 (f) 301.345.1116 (f)
www.recoverynetwork.org

New Vision House of Hope (for Veterans)
410.466.8558
www.newvisionhouseofhope.com

Find. Hope. Here. Dial 988 for emergency emotional support
www.988helpline.org

Reach Health Services
410.752.6080, ext.130
CSHRADER@ibrinc.org

Magruder Action Organization, Inc.
3408 Belair rd. 21213 (410.488.9000, ext.108)
Kcartwright@magrudeactions.com
www.magrudeactions.com

Herbert J. Hoelter Vocational Training Center
301 South Central Avenue Baltimore, Maryland 21202
443.780.1375 (o) 443.865.2459(m)
410.469.9975 (f)
wbillips@ncianet.org
www.ncianet.org

Special Thanks from NCIA

We've been focused on one mission since 1977:

"To help create a society where all persons who come into contact with human service or correctional systems are provided an environment of individual care, concern, and treatment. NCIA is dedicated to developing quality programs and professional services that advocate timely intervention and unconditional care."

With an individual focused and grounded in a community perspective, this social justice mission has remained true for the past four and a half decades. It helped adults with disabilities, youth with disabilities, returning citizens, and SNAP recipients lead fulfilling, meaningful lives that benefit them, their families, and the greater community. We look forward to providing essential disability advocacy, support, and care to continue this mission.

References

Zibaeenezhad, M. J. (2017, December 19). *Comparison of the effect of omega-3 supplements and fresh fish on lipid profile: a randomized, open-labeled trial*. Nature. Retrieved October 13, 2022, from https://www.nature.com/articles/s41387-017-0007-8?error=cookies_not_supported&code=752ef55a-6601-4739-aa6d-06f3dd600083

Petersen, M., Pedersen, H., Major-Pedersen, A., Jensen, T., & Marckmann, P. (2002, October 1). Effect of Fish Oil Versus Corn Oil Supplementation on LDL and HDL Subclasses in Type 2 Diabetic Patients. *Diabetes Care, 25*(10), 1704–1708. https://doi.org/10.2337/diacare.25.10.1704

Eslick, G. D., Howe, P. R., Smith, C., Priest, R., & Bensoussan, A. (2009, July). Benefits of fish oil supplementation in hyperlipidemia: a systematic review and meta-analysis. *International Journal of Cardiology, 136*(1), 4–16. https://doi.org/10.1016/j.ijcard.2008.03.092

Yao, W., Zhang, J. C., Dong, C., Zhuang, C., Hirota, S., Inanaga, K., & Hashimoto, K. (2015, September). Effects of amycenone on serum levels of tumor necrosis factor-α, interleukin-10, and depression-like behavior in mice after lipopolysaccharide administration. *Pharmacology Biochemistry and Behavior*, *136*, 7–12. https://doi.org/10.1016/j.pbb.2015.06.012

Zhang, J., An, S., Hu, W., Teng, M., Wang, X., Qu, Y., Liu, Y., Yuan, Y., & Wang, D. (2016, November 1). The Neuroprotective Properties of Hericium erinaceus in Glutamate-Damaged Differentiated PC12 Cells and an Alzheimer's Disease Mouse Model. *International Journal of Molecular Sciences*, *17*(11), 1810. https://doi.org/10.3390/ijms17111810

Wong, K. H., Naidu, M., David, P., Abdulla, M. A., Abdullah, N., Kuppusamy, U. R., & Sabaratnam, V. (2011). Peripheral Nerve Regeneration FollowiCrush Injury to Rat Peroneal Nerve by Aqueous Extract of Medicinal Mushroom*Hericium erinaceus*(Bull.: Fr) Pers. (Aphyllophoromycetideae). *Evidence-Based Complementary and Alternative Medicine*, *2011*, 1–10. https://doi.org/10.1093/ecam/neq062

Merle, B. M. J., Benlian, P., Puche, N., Bassols, A., Delcourt, C., & Souied, E. H. (2014, March 28). Circulating Omega-3 Fatty Acids and Neovascular Age-Related Macular Degeneration. *Investigative Opthalmology &Amp; Visual Science*, *55*(3), 2010. https://doi.org/10.1167/iovs.14-13916

Yu, D., Shu, X. O., Li, H., Xiang, Y. B., Yang, G., Gao, Y. T., Zheng, W., & Zhang, X. (2013, September 5). Dietary Carbohydrates, Refined Grains, Glycemic Load, and Risk of Coronary Heart Disease in Chinese Adults. *American*

Journal of Epidemiology, *178*(10), 1542–1549. https://doi.org/10.1093/aje/kwt178

Greenwood, D. C., Threapleton, D. E., Evans, C. E., Cleghorn, C. L., Nykjaer, C., Woodhead, C., & Burley, V. J. (2013, November 13). Glycemic Index, Glycemic Load, Carbohydrates, and Type 2 Diabetes. *Diabetes Care*, *36*(12), 4166–4171. https://doi.org/10.2337/dc13-0325

Schulze, M. B. (2004, August 25). Sugar-Sweetened Beverages, Weight Gain, and Incidence of Type 2 Diabetes in Young and Middle-Aged Women. *JAMA*, *292*(8), 927. https://doi.org/10.1001/jama.292.8.927

Wu, X., Beecher, G. R., Holden, J. M., Haytowitz, D. B., Gebhardt, S. E., & Prior, R. L. (2004, May 19). Lipophilic and Hydrophilic Antioxidant Capacities of Common Foods in the United States. *Journal of Agricultural and Food Chemistry*, *52*(12), 4026–4037. https://doi.org/10.1021/jf049696w

De Bont, R. (2004, May 1). Endogenous DNA damage in humans: a review of quantitative data. *Mutagenesis*, *19*(3), 169–185. https://doi.org/10.1093/mutage/geh025

Basu, A., Du, M., Leyva, M. J., Sanchez, K., Betts, N. M., Wu, M., Aston, C. E., & Lyons, T. J. (2010, July 21). Blueberries Decrease Cardiovascular Risk Factors in Obese Men and Women with Metabolic Syndrome. *The Journal of Nutrition*, *140*(9), 1582–1587. https://doi.org/10.3945/jn.110.124701

Johnson, S. A., Figueroa, A., Navaei, N., Wong, A., Kalfon, R., Ormsbee, L. T., Feresin, R. G., Elam, M. L., Hooshmand, S., Payton, M. E., & Arjmandi, B. H. (2015, March). Daily Blueberry Consumption Improves Blood Pressure and Arterial Stiffness in Postmenopausal Women with Pre- and Stage 1-Hypertension: A Randomized, Double-Blind, Placebo-Controlled Clinical Trial. *Journal of the Academy of Nutrition and Dietetics*, *115*(3), 369–377. https://doi.org/10.1016/j.jand.2014.11.001

Popkin, B. M., D'Anci, K. E., & Rosenberg, I. H. (2010, July 20). Water, hydration, and health. *Nutrition Reviews*, *68*(8), 439–458. https://doi.org/10.1111/j.1753-4887.2010.00304.x

Camps, G., Mars, M., de Graaf, C., & Smeets, P. A. (2017, July). A tale of gastric layering and sieving: Gastric emptying of a liquid meal with water blended in or consumed separately. *Physiology &Amp; Behavior*, *176*, 26–30. https://doi.org/10.1016/j.physbeh.2017.03.029

Johnson, R. J., Sánchez-Lozada, L. G., Andrews, P., & Lanaspa, M. A. (2017, May). Perspective: A Historical and Scientific Perspective of Sugar and Its Relation with Obesity and Diabetes. *Advances in Nutrition: An International Review Journal*, *8*(3), 412–422. https://doi.org/10.3945/an.116.014654

Neelakantan, N., Park, S. H., Chen, G. C., & van Dam, R. M. (2021, April 14). Sugar-sweetened beverage consumption, weight gain, and risk of type 2 diabetes and cardiovascular diseases in Asia: a systematic review. *Nutrition Reviews*, *80*(1), 50–67. https://doi.org/10.1093/nutrit/nuab010

Baldwin, H., & Tan, J. (2020, August 3). Effects of Diet on Acne and Its Response to Treatment. *American Journal of Clinical Dermatology*, *22*(1), 55–65. https://doi.org/10.1007/s40257-020-00542-y

Rippe, J., & Angelopoulos, T. (2016, November 4). Relationship between Added Sugars

Consumption and Chronic Disease Risk Factors: Current Understanding. *Nutrients, 8*(11), 697. https://doi.org/10.3390/nu8110697

Martin, M. N., & Ramos, S. (2021, May). Impact of cocoa flavanols on human health. *Food and Chemical Toxicology, 151*, 112121. https://doi.org/10.1016/j.fct.2021.112121

Alkerwi, A., Sauvageot, N., Crichton, G. E., Elias, M. F., & Stranges, S. (2016, March 17). Daily chocolate consumption is inversely associated with insulin resistance and liver enzymes in the Observation of Cardiovascular Risk Factors in Luxembourg study. *British Journal of Nutrition, 115*(9), 1661–1668. https://doi.org/10.1017/s0007114516000702

Ludovici, V., Barthelmes, J., Nägele, M. P., Enseleit, F., Ferri, C., Flammer, A. J., Ruschitzka, F., & Sudano, I. (2017, August 2). Cocoa, Blood Pressure, and Vascular Function. *Frontiers in Nutrition, 4*. https://doi.org/10.3389/fnut.2017.00036

Rippe, J., & Angelopoulos, T. (2016b, November 4). Relationship between Added Sugars Consumption and Chronic Disease Risk Factors: Current Understanding. *Nutrients, 8*(11), 697. https://doi.org/10.3390/nu8110697

Atkinson, F. S., Brand-Miller, J. C., Foster-Powell, K., Buyken, A. E., & Goletzke, J. (2021, July 13). International tables of glycemic index and glycemic load values 2021: a systematic review. *The American Journal of Clinical Nutrition, 114*(5), 1625–1632. https://doi.org/10.1093/ajcn/nqab233

DiNicolantonio, J. J., Lucan, S. C., & O'Keefe, J. H. (2016, March). The Evidence for Saturated Fat and for Sugar Related to Coronary Heart Disease. *Progress in Cardiovascular Diseases*,

58(5), 464–472. https://doi.org/10.1016/j.pcad.2015.11.006

Perera, D. N., Hewavitharana, G. G., & Navaratne, S. B. (2020, July 28). Determination of Physicochemical and Functional Properties of Coconut Oil by Incorporating Bioactive Compounds in Selected Spices. *Journal of Lipids*, *2020*, 1–11. https://doi.org/10.1155/2020/8853940

Genetics and Epigenetics of Addiction DrugFacts. (2022, April 26). National Institute on Drug Abuse. Retrieved October 13, 2022, from https://nida.nih.gov/publications/drugfacts/genetics-epigenetics-addiction

Recovery, G. (2021, June 22). *Why Nutrition & Diet Are Important In Addiction Recovery*. Genesis Recovery. Retrieved October 13, 2022, from https://www.genesisrecovery.com/nutrition-and-diet-in-addiction-recovery/

Keys, 1.2. (2020, February 10). *Key Nutrients and Vitamins You Are Losing While Addicted*. 12 Keys. Retrieved October 13, 2022, from https://www.12keysrehab.com/vitamins-for-addiction-recovery/

Bevilacqua, L., & Goldman, D. (2009, April). Genes and Addictions. *Clinical Pharmacology &Amp; Therapeutics*, *85*(4), 359–361. https://doi.org/10.1038/clpt.2009.6

Lin, T. W., Tsai, S. F., & Kuo, Y. M. (2018, December 12). Physical Exercise Enhances Neuroplasticity and Delays Alzheimer's Disease. *Brain Plasticity*, *4*(1), 95–110. https://doi.org/10.3233/bpl-180073

Fang, R. (2017, January 25). *Music therapy is a potential intervention for cognition of Alzheimer's Disease: a mini-review - Translational Neurodegeneration*. BioMed

Central. Retrieved October 13, 2022, from
https://translationalneurodegeneration.biomedcentral.com/articles/10.1186/s40035-017-0073-9

Made in the USA
Columbia, SC
30 June 2025